MAUSAM

Maritime Cultural Landscapes Across the Indian Ocean

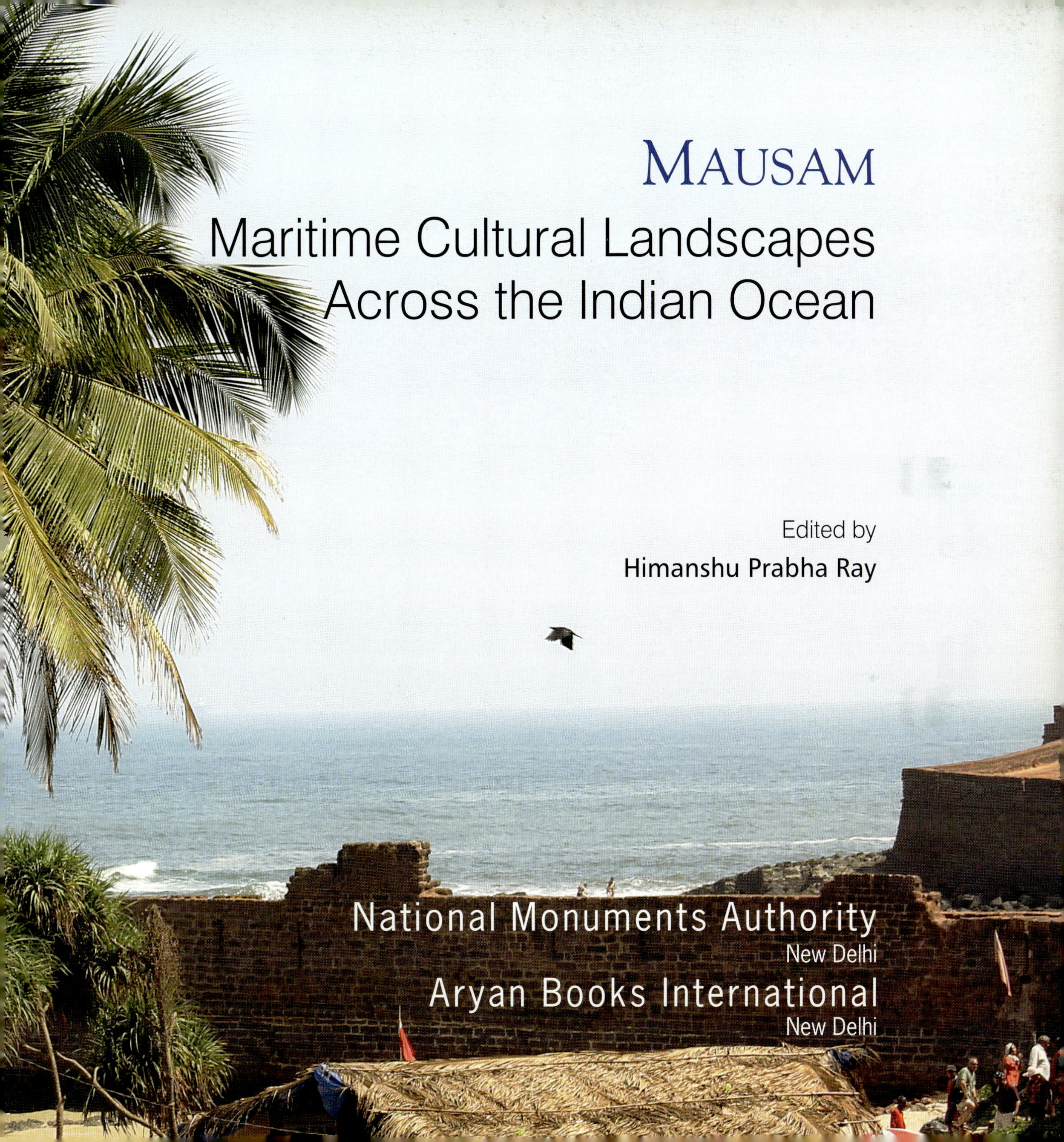

MAUSAM

Maritime Cultural Landscapes Across the Indian Ocean

Edited by

Himanshu Prabha Ray

National Monuments Authority
New Delhi
Aryan Books International
New Delhi

MAUSAM: MARITIME CULTURAL LANDSCAPES ACROSS THE INDIAN OCEAN

ISBN: 978-81-7305-524-9 (HB)
978-81-7305-525-6 (PB)

Responsibility for statements made and visuals provided in the various papers rests solely with the contributors. The views expressed by individual authors are not necessarily those of the editor or of publishers.

Published in **2014** by
National Monuments Authority
24, Tilak Marg, New Delhi - 110 001
www.nma.gov.in
in association with
Aryan Books International
Pooja Apartments, 4B, Ansari Road, New Delhi - 110 002
Tel.: 23287589, 23255799; Fax: 91-11-23270385
E-mail: aryanbooks@gmail.com
www.aryanbooks.co.in

Designed and Printed in India by ABI Prints & Publishing Co., New Delhi.

Preface

Mausam: Blueprint for Reviving Traditional Networks

The papers in this book were presented in New Delhi as a part of an ongoing dialogue among scholars and researchers from different disciplines on maritime cultural landscapes, as these evolved across the Indian Ocean both spatially and historically. A common concern that all papers share is with definitions of maritime spaces; different articulations of social and political power; regional and local nautical traditions; and diverse environmental niches. 'Mausam' or Arabic 'Mawsim' refers to the season when ships could sail safely. This distinctive wind-system of the Indian Ocean region follows a regular pattern: southwest from May to September; and northeast from November to March. The English term 'Monsoon' came from Portuguese 'Monção', ostensibly from Arabic 'Mawsim'. The etymology of this word signifies the importance of this season to a variety of seafarers. This intertwining of natural phenomena such as monsoon winds and the ways in which these were harnessed historically to create cultural networks provide building blocks for contemporary societies, as they work towards universal values and trans-border groupings—both of which underwrite UNESCO's 1972 World Heritage Convention. As World History acquires centrality and the focus shifts from national histories to globalisation, the history of the sea is discussed as 'connected history' across porous borders, linked through boat-building traditions, community networks and cultural practices (Vink, 2007: 41-62).

Thus the endeavour of Project Mausam is to position itself at two levels: at the macro level it aims to re-connect and re-establish communications between countries of the Indian Ocean world, which would lead to an enhanced understanding of cultural values and concerns; while at the micro level the focus will be on understanding national cultures in their regional maritime milieu. This two-fold emphasis is important if issues related to local communities, regional governance and the management of heritage sites are to be included in the discussion.

Historical Background

The 'discovery' of the etesian or annual winds is attributed to the Greeks, although Indian and Arab sailors are known to have used the monsoon winds much earlier. This regular pattern facilitated the movement of people, goods and ideas across the Indian Ocean,

enabling cultural interactions and exchange until when steam-powered cargo carriers reduced reliance on sailing ships. These ancient connections were not limited to the coastal regions; they pervaded life in the hinterland and impacted inland communities as well.

This book focuses on how this natural phenomenon has shaped interactions between countries and communities connected by the Indian Ocean. The knowledge and use of the monsoon impacted ancient and historical trade, local economies, religion, politics and cultural identity. Centuries of trade, migration, colonialism and modern statecraft transformed these traditional interactions across the Indian Ocean, but present-day national identities and perceptions of the past are deeply interwoven with age-old ties.

Fishermen, sailors and merchants travelled the waters of the Indian Ocean as early as the third millennium BCE, linking the world's earliest civilizations from Africa to East Asia in a complex web of relationships. The commodities exchanged through these networks included a wide array of objects—aromatics, medicines, dyes, spices, grain, wood, textiles, gems, stones and ornaments, metals, and plant and animal products—and were transported through voyages and sold at markets or bazaars along the Indian Ocean littoral. Many of the commodities involved had multiple meanings and diverse functions. Spices, for example, were not only used as condiments and for preservation of food, but also played a major role in *materia medica* and ritual practices. Additionally, while trade might have underpinned many of these cross-cultural relationships, the Ocean was also a highway for the exchange of religious cultures and specialized technologies. The expansion of Hinduism, Buddhism, Islam and Christianity helped define the boundaries of this Indian Ocean 'world', creating networks of religious travel and pilgrimage. The construction of traditional sailing craft involved trade and transportation of wood for planking and coconut coir for stitching from different regions of the Indian Ocean, enabling the transmission and preservation of ancient boat-building technologies.

How was exchange across the Indian Ocean organized? There are multiple sources that help us answer this question; ranging from archaeological evidence to inscriptions and textual references from a range of time periods. Examples of such trade, exchange and interaction abound in the Indian Ocean world, ranging from third-millennium BCE Harappan ceramics, beads, and seals found on sites across the Arabian peninsula to accounts of European sailors travelling the seas in the nineteenth-century. Maritime voyages in the early centuries of the Common Era were regarded as profitable ventures and Buddhist literature describes a variety of social groups who were involved. In addition to merchants there are references to princes who travelled across the seas to make money. The prosperity and status of these mariners is evident from the donations made by them to the Buddhist monastic establishments, along the coasts of the Indian Ocean and recorded in inscriptions of the Early Historic period.

Temples and monasteries were not merely centres of devotion and worship, but were also principal institutions in the medieval period for establishing laws and enforcing them on their members. A large number of inscriptions from early medieval India document complex arrangements for the use of temple resources, whether these were lands or else revenues from shops and markets. In the larger temples, we find mention of several classes of temple employees such as administrators, treasurers, accountants, temple women, cooks, sweepers, artisans, watchmen, etc. Resources for temple rituals and for the large number of employees were generated through surplus agricultural production on temple lands and from donations in cash and kind from trading groups. The inscriptions also provide a record of legal transactions conducted and in addition to the temple archives on income and expenditure form a valuable source of information on the legal jurisdiction of the temple. A good example of this is the study of the early seventeenth century archives of a temple in Kerala.

One of the characteristic features of maritime trade from the ninth-tenth centuries onwards was the location of markets in fortified settlements along the Indian Ocean littoral and farther inland. Rules governing the payment of taxes and regulating the functioning of the markets were often inscribed on copper plates and provide useful insights into the organization of the trade network. The Kollam copper plates of Sthanu Ravi from the Malabar coast are significant in connection with trading rights granted to the Christian church. A market was located within the precincts of the fortified settlement at the coastal centre of Kollam, while the church was situated outside the fortification wall.

Another aspect of the maritime networks relates to the visual topography that provided landmarks to sailors and defined the sailing world in antiquity. "The chains of perceptibility created by looking from one vantage point to the next served both to express the relationship of individual localities to one another and to make sense of the wider world" (Horden and Purcell 2000: 125). This visual topography was characterized by coastal structures, many of them religious in nature that created a distinctive maritime milieu. For example, the thirteenth-century Konark Temple on the coast of Odisha in India was known as the 'Black Pagoda' to European sailors, as opposed to the 'White Pagoda', the Jagannath Temple in Puri. Similarly, the Buddhist temple at Nagapattinam on the Tamil coast in India, erected for Chinese Buddhists, was a major landmark for ships from the seventh to the nineteenth centuries when it was demolished by French Jesuits.

How does an understanding of the maritime heritage of countries around the Indian Ocean littoral provide a viable model to deepen the knowledge of their own cultural legacy, while at the same time engaging with trans-oceanic networks? Legislation and measures for preservation require identification and documentation of the maritime heritage in local and regional contexts. More importantly, its protection draws on national agendas. Can a balance be achieved between national interests and trans-national research collaboration? In the final section, it is suggested that UNESCO's World Heritage Convention has broadened its appeal over the years to incorporate a variety of interests.

The Future: Cultural Maritime Routes and Trans-national Nominations

The General Conference of the UNESCO in 1972 adopted a Convention concerning Protection of World Cultural and Natural Heritage. The Convention sought to encourage the identification, protection and preservation of cultural and natural heritage around the world considered to be of outstanding value to humanity. India ratified this Convention in November 1977. The Archaeological Survey of India (ASI) functions as a nodal agency for nomination of World Heritage Sites (WHS) to the UNESCO. In addition, it has been involved in conservation work in several countries of the region.

Another step in promoting capacity building in the region involves the establishment of the Category 2 Centre (C2C) proposed by India. This has been envisioned to be a centre of excellence for the conservation of natural and cultural heritage in Asia Pacific Region. It will perform a catalytic role in India and the countries in the Asia region by training and researching issues involved with World Heritage Sites (WHS) inscription, protection, conservation, monitoring and management. The scope of the proposed Centre will therefore be global, regional, and interregional to bring greater synergy to the conservation and management of World Heritage Sites in particular but also other heritage sites in general.

According to the decision of the World Heritage Committee at its 29th session held at Durban in 2005, it was agreed to be 'aware of the need to specify the submission modalities for the nomination of transboundary or transnational serial properties on the World Heritage List'. Categories of heritage within the framework of the World Heritage Convention have been broadened over the decades to include cultural landscapes, industrial remains, and heritage routes, which are all now valued as part of our cultural heritage. The World Heritage Committee has also reflected upon such subjects as the need for community involvement, social benefits, heritage as part of sustainable development and the engagement of young people in the World Heritage process (http://whc.unesco.org/archive/2005/whc05-29com-inf09Ae.pdf accessed on 10th May 2014, p. 15). The UNESCO Universal Declaration of Cultural Diversity, adopted in November 2001, states "Culture takes diverse forms across time and space. This diversity is embodied in the uniqueness and plurality of the identities of the groups and societies making up humankind. As a source of exchange, innovation and creativity, cultural diversity is as necessary for humankind as biodiversity is for nature".

Project Mausam aims to promote research on themes related to the study of Maritime Cultural Routes through international scientific seminars and meetings and by adopting a multidisciplinary approach. It will encourage the production of specialized works, as well as publications for the general public with an attempt at promoting a broader understanding of the concept of a common heritage and multiple identities.

References

Horden, P. and Nicholas Purcell, *The Corrupting Sea: A Study of Mediterranean History*, Oxford: Blackwell, 2000.

Vink, Markus, Indian Ocean Studies and the 'New Thalassology', *Journal of Global History*, 2, (2007): 41-62.

Contents

List of Illustrations

1

Maritime Landscapes and Coastal Architecture: The Long Coastline of India

Himanshu Prabha Ray

The Indian Ocean presented a unique environment to the sailor in antiquity. To sail in this region, the ships had to be "good weatherly sailors, fast, good carriers, deep-drafted and able to go to windward as well. In short they had to be *real* sailing ships" (Villiers 1952: 56-57). The monsoon winds not only determined the basic rhythm for seafaring activity across much of tropical and equatorial Asia, but also influenced agricultural activity in the region. Historians have long accepted that the 'world's largest area of monsoonal tropics, shares a pattern of rainforest and water which provided a background for all . . . economic and social activity' (Reid 2001: 218). This essay suggests that one way of understanding this complex web of interactions of the past is through a deep engagement with markers of maritime regions and the communities that inhabited these spaces. The indicators include archaeological artefacts, as evidence of ancient settlements and routes, architectural edifices and their networks of interaction and of course, continuing boat-building traditions.

The larger issue addressed here relates to perspectives through which monuments, especially those located on the coast are to be understood and made meaningful to contemporary societies, both for an appreciation of their aesthetic value, as also to aid in their preservation for posterity. Monuments in Asia have generally been studied in terms of architecture and sculpture or with regard to chronology and patronage and more recently within debates of generation of colonial knowledge, but seldom with regard to cultural plurality and diversity and/or historical memory. Monuments enshrine many kinds of memories: memory of the vision of the builder; memory acquired over time; and finally, the created memory through transformation of the monument, either owing to its destruction or by altering its context or form. Monuments also become sites for enactment of rituals such as pilgrimage for the replenishment of memory and knowledge of the past.

The attempt in this essay is to articulate the complex connections built through the mediation of the sea both spatially and chronologically by an examination of coastal architecture in India. The focus here is on the historical period, as other papers in this book discuss the prehistoric past (cf. the essays by Yaduvir Singh Rawat and Akshyeta Suryanarayan). We start with a discussion of the architectural evidence for habitation in coastal zones in the historical period; and contrast this with an active engagement and contestation over maritime space as reflected in inscriptions. In the final section, we present an overview of the varied conceptualizations of the sea in textual narratives and juxtapose these with sculptural representations on religious architecture. We discuss this issue through representations of the concept of a saviour from troubles at sea, which are found at several Buddhist monastic sites and are depicted at both coastal and inland sites in South and Southeast Asia. These examples underscore the enormous reach of the sea, both as a physical space as well as entity that has long affected the human psyche.

Traditionally, the navigators of the Indian Ocean learnt their routes by identifying natural phenomena and by checking their positions by stars. Certain routes across the Indian Ocean were more feasible than others were and continued to be in use in the historical period. Stellar navigation made sailing along the latitude possible, though finding the longitude was relatively more difficult. However, longitude tables were theoretically prepared by mathematical computations and early versions of nautical charts were perhaps available for specific routes and sailing schedules. This mapping and remapping of the Indian Ocean across two millennia is important for Project Mausam, especially in an age prior to the encapsulation of this oceanic space through maps and nautical charts. This has been discussed with reference to coastal Vietnam elsewhere in this book (cf. the essay by Tran Ky Phuong). In this paper, the focus is on the India and both the west and east coasts, as discussed in the next section.

Seascapes and the Coastline of India

The demarcation of seascapes may be understood through intellectual traditions of writing, but more importantly through an active engagement with the nature of coastal installations that physically circumscribed the seafaring world. In the 1950s, the Swedish maritime ethnologist Olof Hasslof introduced the term *sjobruk* or maritime cultural landscape signifying demarcation and utilisation of maritime space by communities for settlement, fishing, shipping, pilotage, etc. (Westerdahl 1992: 5). The Indian Ocean is perhaps one of the few regions where this concept can be applied for an understanding of maritime history and archaeology on account of the continued survival of maritime regions. These regions have participated historically in the Indian Ocean network and in several cases are characterised by local traditions of boat building and navigation, architectural features and archaeological sites, as well as narratives of the central experience of trans-locality of maritime communities. Thus it is important to comprehend conceptions of the sea by people who lived along its coasts and traversed it for a variety of reasons.

The Architectural Testimony of the West Coast

The Western Coastal Plain is best described as a narrow strip of land between the hills of the Western Ghats on the east and the Arabian Sea on the west (Fig. 1.1). It ranges in width from 50 to 100 kilometres and extends from the present state of Gujarat in the north through Maharashtra, Goa, Karnataka, and Kerala. Numerous rivers cut across the region. Mostly originating in the Western Ghats, the rivers are fast-flowing, usually perennial, and empty into estuaries.

The starting point for this discussion is Gujarat marked by a long coastline from the Gulf of Kachchh to the Gulf of Cambay and characterised by mud flats and saline wastes. In the coastal regions of Gujarat, Buddhist caves were excavated from second century BCE to the sixth century CE. Rock-cut caves are known from Kateshwar and five from Siyot in Lakhpat taluka in the extreme north-west of Kachchh. Other coastal sites in south Gujarat include Talaja in Bhavnagar district with thirty rock-cut caves (Fig. 1.2) and Kadia Dungar near Bharuch.

Valabhi located on the Bhavnagar creek, at the head of the Gulf of Cambay, emerged not

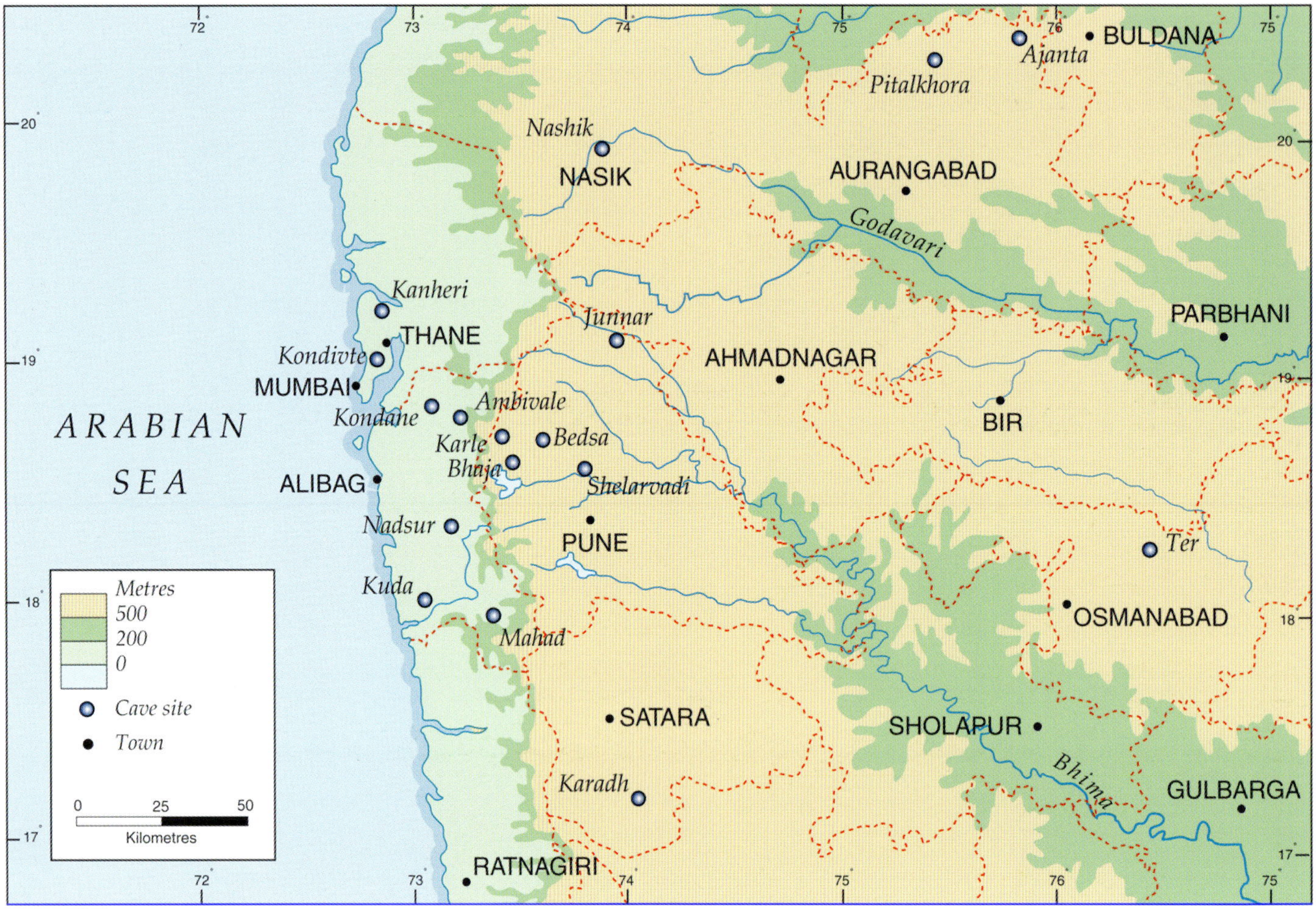

Fig. 1.1. Map of the Western Deccan showing locations of early Buddhist sites.

merely as an outlet for maritime trade, but also as the capital of the ruling dynasty of Maitrakas (493 – 776 CE) and the core area for religious consolidation. Contemporary Sanskrit literature such as the literary work the *Daśakumāracaritam* by Dandin describes Valabhi as a prosperous trading centre, where the chief of sea-traders lived (Kale, 1986: 164, 332). References to its wealthy resident and travelling communities of traders are also found in the

Fig. 1.2. Caves cut in the side of the hill at Talaja with modern Jain temple on top.

copper plate inscriptions from the reign of the Hepthalite ruler Toramana whose kingdom extended over north-western and western India in the late fifth and early sixth centuries CE (Mehta and Thakkar 1978).

More than a thousand Buddhist caves were excavated in the hills of the Western Ghats and its offshoots at about fifty centres in the present state of Maharashtra, from the second century BCE onward. Broadly these sites are located overlooking creeks and coastal settlements and at passes along overland routes. Of these, nineteen centres are significant in terms of providing inscriptional data and have yielded a total of more than two hundred inscriptions (Ray 1986). Of these Kanheri near the present city of Mumbai was the largest religious centre along the west coast of India with one hundred and four caves located in the fertile basin of the Ulhas river dated from first to eleventh century CE. There are three eleventh century inscriptions in cave 90 in the Pahlavi script, which is a writing system adopted for various Middle Iranian languages (Gokhale 1991, 142).

A trend that is relevant to the reconstruction of coastal landscapes relates to shifts in coastal centres over time, for example between the ports of Bharuch, Sopara, Kalyan, Chaul and Surat—all located on the Konkan coast in the present states of Gujarat and Maharashtra. These shifts were linked both to silting of river mouths where the centres were located, as well as to changes in internal routes linking the coast to the capitals and cities of the interior. It was only with the transformation of the motley collection of seven islands with a variety of landing places into the port of Bombay in the nineteenth century that an identifiable and permanent port city was created on the west coast of India. Until this transformation, several landing places had been in existence in the vicinity of Bombay.

Moving south, the coastal belt of Karnataka extends to about 10 to 20 kilometres inland and is rich in mineral resources such as iron, copper, limestone, mica, gold, garnet, etc. An early site on the Kanara coast was Chandor or Chandrapura on the river Paroda leading to the sea. Archaeological excavations conducted at the site of Chandor (ancient Chandrapura) in district South Goa have exposed the complete plan of a brick temple complex datable from fourth to eleventh century CE. Cosmas Indicopleustes, the sixth century native of Alexandria who travelled to India and Sri Lanka, refers to a series of coastal centres in his *Christian Topography* (Wolska-Conus 1968-73, Book XI: 367-68), especially on the Karnataka and Kerala coasts. The coastal belt of Kerala extending over 580 kilometres is relatively flat, teeming with paddy fields, coconut groves and is crisscrossed by a network of interconnected canals and rivers.

Forts were other important structures that played a major role in the demarcation of the visual topography in the Indian Ocean from the ninth to tenth centuries onwards. Unfortunately there is very little that remains of these earlier fortified settlements and a majority of the present forts date from the thirteenth century onwards

(Naravane 1998, 127). The presence of fortified settlements along the coast should be seen in the context of emerging trade guilds with operations across the Indian Ocean who forged close links with royal houses. The most prominent in peninsular India was the Ayyavole beginning from the eighth or ninth century to the seventeenth century, while others included the Manigramam, and several other merchant groups (Abraham 1988). Thus a very different sailing regime from that functioning at present was in place. This was also reflected in the modest nature of coastal centres as compared to the present metropolises of Mumbai or Goa. The west coast also provides for a different engagement with the sea when compared to the east coast of India, as discussed in the next section.

The Archaeology of the East Coast of India

The Bay of Bengal forms the north-eastern part of the Indian Ocean bordered on the east by Burma and the Malay peninsula and on the west by India. The southern extremes reach the island of Sri Lanka, and the Andaman and Nicobar Islands. It is beyond these islands that the waters of the Bay of Bengal merge with those of the South China Sea that extends from the Malacca Straits to the Strait of Taiwan encompassing the coasts of Thailand, Vietnam (cf. Tran Ky Phuong in this volume) and south China. In this section, the discussion is limited to the coastal regions of India and mainly to the present states of Odisha, Andhra and Tamil Nadu (Fig. 1.3).

In the second-first millennium BCE peninsular India was home to iron-using megalithic communities and social integration was measured through the construction of large monuments of stone, often sepulchral in nature. Chronologically, the Iron Age megalithic sites span several centuries from 1200 BCE to 300 CE and extend across all regions of peninsular India, including along the coasts. The presence of Megalithic sites is evident along the river Krishna, as also along the Andhra and Tamil coasts. In addition to the inland network, there are indications for the participation of these Iron Age communities in a wider trading network incorporating sites in north India as well as those in Sri Lanka (Ray 1994, Chapter II).

Starting from modest beginnings in the third century BCE, the east coast is marked by large Buddhist monastic complexes overlooking the sea. Recent archaeological research has brought to light several Buddhist sites in Odisha, though the major expansion occurred from the fifth to thirteenth centuries CE, when more than one hundred Buddhist sites are known in the region.

Fig. 1.3. Map of the Eastern Deccan showing sites with Buddhist monastic complexes along the coast.

Nearly 140 Buddhist sites are listed along the Andhra region dating from the second century BCE onwards and the distribution along the coast from Srikakulam in the north to Ramatirtham and Nandalur in the south is quite striking. Of these, thirty Buddhist sites have yielded stone inscriptions recording donations made by a cross-section of the populace to the Buddhist Sangha or community of monks.

Arikamedu, 4 kilometres south of Pondicherry on the Tamil coast, is perhaps one of the few historical sites that have been subjected to several seasons of archaeological excavations starting from 1941 onward. One of the early excavators, Mortimer Wheeler had suggested that the site was abandoned with the decline of Roman trade in the second century CE. This idea has changed as a result of more recent work conducted between 1989 and 1992, which has provided evidence for the continuation of the site well into the tenth-eleventh centuries CE (Begley et al., 1996, 1). The settlement at Arikamedu grew along the river bank and the impetus for its growth was provided by trade, with fish being one of the traded items along with pepper, salt and paddy.

An issue that requires consideration at this stage relates to the extent and vigour of the trading network linking eastern India with the Bay of Bengal and evidence for the spread of Buddhism across the Ocean. A cluster of fifth century inscriptions of unequivocal Buddhist affiliation was found in Kedah on the west coast of the Malay peninsula. Three of these inscriptions are made of local stone and bear similar illustrations of Buddhist stupas. Texts very similar to these inscriptions have been found on the island of Borneo and on the coast of Brunei (Christie 1995, 256). The most interesting of these inscriptions in Sanskrit, refers to the setting up of the stone by the mariner Buddhagupta, resident of Raktamrttika, identified with Rajbadidanga in Bengal, on the successful completion of his voyage (Fig. 1.4) (Chhabra 1965, 23-24).

There was a shift in maritime networks around the middle of the first millennium CE and pilgrims visiting sites associated with the life of the Buddha formed a major category of travellers. The Chinese pilgrim Faxian arrived overland in India in 399 CE and returned by sea to China in 413-414 CE from Sri Lanka heading towards the northwest tip of Sumatra. The ship was wrecked on the way and perhaps landed in the Andamans. The next phase took Faxian to the northwest of Borneo where he arrived in 414 CE after 90 days at sea. The pilgrim remained in Borneo for five months and then left for China in mid-414 CE heading towards Canton.

Perhaps the most relevant example for this paper is the Buddhist monastery at Nagapattinam, which was a major landmark on the Tamil coast from the seventh to the nineteenth centuries CE. A Buddhist temple was erected at Nagapattinam specifically for Chinese Buddhists at the instance of a Chinese ruler during the reign of the Pallava ruler Narasimhavarman II (*c.* CE 695–722). The Chinese monk Wu-hing visited the site on his way to Sri Lanka (Ramachandran 1954: 14). One of the later Srivijayan kings, perhaps from the island of Sumatra, Maravijayottungavarman, is known

Fig. 1.4. Buddhagupta inscription set up on the west coast of the Malay peninsula on successful completion of the voyage, now in the Indian Museum, Kolkata.

to have provided for the construction of the temple. Revenues of a large village Anaimangalam were granted for its upkeep in 1006 CE by the ruler of the Chola dynasty of south India, King Rajaraja I.

Sir Walter Elliot (1803-1887), a Scottish civil servant in India, visited the Chinese Pagoda, as the site was then known, in 1846 on board the government steamer *Hugh Lindsay*, which travelled down the coast. Elliot described the structure at Nagapattinam as a "four-sided tower of three stories constructed of bricks closely fitted together without cement" (Elliot 1878, 224). There was a fort in its vicinity and, "about 11/3 miles NNW from the fort stands the old Black Pagoda, which is one of the most conspicuous objects in approaching this part of the coast, the whole of which has a low, drowned aspect when first seen from the offing, consisting as it does of a sandy barren soil planted with coconut trees" (Horsburgh 1817, 453). It may be mentioned that Nagapattinam was also the terminus of the great south Indian railway and an important landmark for the large numbers of ships and steamers travelling to the roadstead. As a depressing commentary of colonial policies, in spite of local objections, the governor-in-Council approved the demolition of the Buddhist monastery on 28 August 1867 by French Jesuits who had been expelled from

Pondicherry and had wanted to construct a college in its place.

After this brief overview of architecture along the east coast, we shift the discussion to explaining the engagement of the political elite with the sea in the next section.

The Sea as Contested Space

By the second-first century BCE, royal inscriptions initiate the practice of defining the domain of a king. Thus the inscription of Balasiri, mother of one of the early kings of the Satavahana dynasty who ruled over large parts of the Deccan in the early centuries of the Common Era, Gotamiputa Siri Satakani, while recording the gift of a cave to the Buddhist Sangha, also mentions honorific titles of the king to indicate his sovereignty over a vast territory stretching until the three oceans. This is a practice that continues into later periods. While describing the history of the early Chalukya dynasty of western India, the seventh century inscription refers to Mangalisa, whose army was powerful enough to invade all islands, crossed the ocean by bridges of boats and effected the plundering of the island of Revati (Fleet 1879, 13).

The Silahara kings who ruled over large parts of western India around the present city of Mumbai from 810 to 1240 regularly refer to themselves as lord of the western ocean (Mirashi, 1977, 127-30). The 11th century Panjim plates mention King Guhalla Deva of the Goa Kadambas as undertaking a pilgrimage to Somnath on the Gujarat coast, but he had hardly reached halfway when the mast of his ship broke and he was forced to take shelter with a ruler friendly to him at the port of Goa (Moraes 1995, 171), where a rich Muslim merchant by the name of Madumod, of Taji origin and the wealthiest of all the seafaring traders, came to the help of the king. In return, the king rewarded him with a lot of wealth. This record tells us for the first time of Arab traders settled on the Goa coast in 11th century CE. Clearly then maritime space formed an integral part of political thinking and conceptualization of the inhabited world—a world that was certainly claimed, but not always controlled.

To what extent did attempts to enforce political authority lead to conflict across the Ocean? A response to this issue is evident from an examination of hero stones found on the west coast of India. These were raised in memory of those who lost their lives in sea-battles and are dated from twelfth to fifteenth century CE. Four of the hero stones are housed in the Archaeological Museum of Goa and depict double-ended vessels propelled by oars, very similar to those known from the region at present. The ships are crowded with soldiers armed with bows and engaged in fights (Figs. 1.5–1.6).

Clearly, there is a long history of conflict across the Ocean. At the same time, the sea is also conceptualized as a fearsome space. This leads to the next section where we shift the focus to the seafarer and the trials and tribulations so graphically depicted in textual accounts, but also represented on early religious architecture not only along the coasts, but inland as well.

The Saviour of the Sailor

The ocean evoked varied feelings in those who lived on its shores and those who traversed it. These are graphically depicted in poems included in the anthology of four hundred poems in Old Tamil of the early centuries of the Common Era (Hart and Heifetz 1999, 189-90) and are also portrayed on monuments. In the previous section we have referred to depictions of sea battles on memorial stones. In addition to these, there are sculptural reliefs on monuments of Buddhist monastic complexes both along the coasts, as also inland that deal with issues of ship-wreck and emphasize the power of believing in the Bodhisattva Avalokitesvara who is graphically shown as saving the devotee from several troubles, including ship-wreck. These references reflect an engagement with the sea, in its benign

Fig. 1.5. 12th century hero stone from the Archaeological Museum, Goa.

Fig. 1.6. 14th century hero stone now in the Archaeological Museum, Goa.

as well as malevolent form not only by merchants and trading groups, but also fishing and sailing communities and ship captains who carried cargoes across the waters.

The emergence of the cult of the Bodhisattva Avalokitesvara as a saviour of mariners and travellers in distress is generally associated with the Lotus Sutra (*Saddharmapuṇḍarīka Sūtra*), which was translated into Chinese in the third century CE and became very influential in the countries of Southeast Asia. The scene of Bodhisattva as Saviour was also sculpted prominently at a large number of Buddhist monastic sites. Several renditions were made in the rock-cut caves of the western Deccan and over twelve painted and/or sculpted versions are known from the World Heritage site of Ajanta (caves 2, 4, 6, 10A, 11, 17, 20, 26), three from Kanheri (caves 2, 41 and 90), one from Aurangabad (cave 7) and two from the caves at Ellora near Aurangabad, though nowhere is the composition so elaborate and the treatment so elegant as in cave 90 at Kanheri. The image in cave 90 of Bodhisattva Avalokitesvara, offers the devotee promise of salvation from the various perils depicted at the sides of the composition including attack by elephants, lions, robbers and of course ship wreck (Huntington 1993, 264-65).

In one of his previous births, Sakyamuni Gautama was born as Simhala, a merchant who led five hundred others on a seagoing venture to Tamradvipa or Sri Lanka. They were shipwrecked, but eventually saved from the man-eating ogresses by the horse Balaha, who rose majestically into the sky with Simhala on his back. The ogresses, however, followed him back to his kingdom. Simhala once again rose to the occasion and saved the kingdom from being devoured by them. Simhala was crowned king and Tamradvipa was renamed Simhaladvipa (Holt 1991, 49-50). The story of the horse Balaha as saviour of merchants is prominently shown on a pillar from the site of Mathura, situated about 150 kilometres south of Delhi (Fig. 1.7), as also at sites in Cambodia and Indonesia. Representations of sea travel from Neak Pean in Angkor and Borobudur in central Java are also relevant for this paper. Neak Pean is a small island temple located in the middle of the last baray (the Preah Khan Baray or Jayatataka) constructed by a Khmer king in the Angkor area. The temple is faced by a much-damaged sculpture of the horse, Balaha, saving drowning sailors (Fig. 1.8).

Fig. 1.7. Relief depicting Balahasa Jataka on railing pillar from Mathura.

In the rock cut shrines at Ellora close to Aurangabad, the function of the Avalokitesvara as the saviour from the eight perils is delegated to the female deity Tara in cave 9. This theme occurs prominently in the monastic establishment at Ratnagiri in Odisha. Ratnagiri is a 25 metre high isolated hill of khondalite formation of the Assia range bounded on three sides by the rivers Brahmani, the Kimiria and the Birupa and local tradition refers to the region as being close to the sea in the past. Two standing images of Tara as saviour from the eight perils

Fig. 1.8. Balahasa Jataka from the Buddhist temple at Neak Pean, Angkor.

were found from the surface at Ratnagiri. One of the standing images, now in Patna museum, dates to the end of the 8th century CE and shows Tara flanked by scenes of the eight perils depicted in two vertical rows of four panels each (Fig. 1.9) (Mitra 1983, 444-45). A second image is dated to the 11th century on the basis of a fragmentary inscription and graphically portrays the fear of drowning in a sinking boat (Fig. 1.10) (Mitra 1983, 428).

In the final analysis, the maritime orientation of many of the shrines and forts discussed in this paper is evident. Histories written over the last five decades in different countries have primarily dealt with the period of the present nation-states and the discussion has largely centred on present

Fig. 1.9. 8th century standing image of Tara from Ratnagiri now in the Patna Museum.

Fig. 1.10. Standing Tara image in Site Museum, Ratnagiri.

national boundaries and local identities versus external influences. Perhaps it is time to move beyond the paradigm of the nation-state in researching the history of the sea as these frontiers had little meaning in the earlier period.

It is also important that Project Mausam should create an awareness of the maritime heritage of the Indian Ocean so that some of the earlier links could again become a part of the enduring legacy of travel across the Indian Ocean. No doubt, ideas about religious and ethnic identities often draw from prevailing notions of the past and it is here that the present and the past are inextricably linked not only to individual destinies, but more significantly to the larger meta-narratives of the nation states or as in recent years, the globalising world. A leading historian of Southeast Asia, Oliver Wolters, succinctly states that the purpose of history and the study of the past could well be an enhancement of self-awareness and a better understanding of the present (Wolters 1994, 2).

By focusing on nautical histories, architecture and archaeology, on the central experience of trans-locality of maritime communities and the mapping and remapping of maritime conceptions of space across two millennia, the project reorients the audience from the conventional linear imperial construct of maritime history as domination, conflict and control to looking at the reality of constant cultural transfer and transmission within the domain of the Indian Ocean world.

References

Abraham, Meera, *Two Medieval Merchant Guilds of South India*, New Delhi: Manohar, 1988.

Begley, Vimala, The Ancient Port of Arikamedu: New Excavations and Researches 1989-1992, *Mémoires Archéologiques* 22 (1996): 351-68. Pondichéry: Ecole française d'Extrême Orient.

Chhabra, Bahadur Chand, *Expansion of the Indo-Aryan Culture during Pallava Rule*, Delhi: Munshiram Manoharlal, 1965.

Christie, Jan W., State Formation in Early Maritime Southeast Asia: A Consideration of the Theories and the Data, *Bijdragen tot de Taal-, Land- en Volkenkunde*, 151, 2 (1995): 235-88.

Elliot, Sir Walter, The Edifice Formerly Known as the Chinese or Jain Pagoda at Negapatanam, *Indian Antiquary* 7 (1878): 224-27.

Fleet, J.F., Sanskrit and Old Canarese Inscriptions, *Indian Antiquary* VIII (1879): 10-15; 284-85.

Gokhale, Shobhana, *Kanheri Inscriptions,* Pune: Deccan College Post Graduate and Research Institute, 1991.

Hart, George L. and Hank Heifetz, *The Four Hundred Songs of War and Wisdom: An Anthology of Poems from Classical Tamil,* New York: Columbia University Press, 1999.

Holt, John C., *Buddha in the Crown: Avalokitesvara in the Buddhist Traditions of Sri Lanka,* New York: Oxford University Press, 1991.

Horsburgh, James, *A Compendium or Epitome of Winds, Weather, Waves, Luminous Appearance, and Temperature of the Sea, Magnetism, Variation of the Compass, Chronometers, Coral*

Formations, Swimming and Security in Lading Ships, London: Black, Parbury and Allen, 1817.

Huntington, Susan L., *The Art of Ancient India: Buddhist, Hindu, Jaina*, New York, Tokyo: Weatherhill, 1993.

Kale, M.R. (ed.), *Dasakumaracarita of Dandin*, Delhi: Motilal Banarsidass, 1986.

Kempers, A.J. Bernet, *Ageless Borobudur*, Wassenaar: Servire, 1976.

Mehta, Ramanlal N. and A.M. Thakkar, *M.S. University Copper Plates of the Time of Toramana*, Vadodara: Maharaja Sayaji Rao University, 1978.

Mitra, Debala, *Ratnagiri (1958-61), Memoirs of the Archaeological Survey of India* 80, Volume 1, New Delhi: Archaeological Survey of India (1981).

Mitra, Debala, *Ratnagiri (1958-61), Memoirs of the Archaeological Survey of India* 80, Volume 2, New Delhi: Archaeological Survey of India (1983).

Moraes, George M., *The Kadamba Kula: A History of Ancient and Medieval Karnataka*, Madras: Asian Education Services, 1995.

Naravane, M.S., Restoration, Preservation and Utilization of the Coastal Forts of India, in Philippe la Hausse de Lalouvière (ed.), *Coastal Fortifications*, pp. 126-31. Tamarin, Mauritius: Heritage, 1998.

Ray, Himanshu Prabha, *Monastery and Guild: Commerce under the Satavahanas*, New Delhi: Oxford University Press, 1986.

——, *The Winds of Change: Buddhism and the Maritime Links of Early South Asia*, New Delhi: Oxford University Press, 1994.

Ramachandran, T.N., The Nagapattinam and Other Buddhist Bronzes in the Madras Museum, *Bulletin of the Madras Museum* 7, 1 (1954).

Reid, Anthony, Humans and Forests in Pre-Colonial Southeast Asia, in J.R. McNeill (ed.), *Environmental History in the Pacific World*, pp. 218, Aldershot, UK: Ashgate, 2001.

Schlingloff, Dietler, *Studies in Ajanta Paintings: Identifications and Interpretations*, Columbia, Missourie: South Asia Books, 1988.

Spink, Walter M., *Ajanta: History and Development, Cave by Cave*, Volume IV, Leiden: Brill, 2007.

Spink, Walter M., Ajanta: History and Development, *Painting, Sculpture, Architecture*, Volume V, Leiden: Brill, 2009.

Villiers, Alan, *Monsoon Seas: The Story of the Indian Ocean*, New York: Mcgraw-Hill, 1952.

Westerdahl, Christer, The Maritime Cultural Landscape, *The International Journal of Nautical Archaeology* 21.1(1992): 5-14.

Wolska-Conus, Wanda, *Cosmas Indicopleustes, Topographie Chrétienne*, 3 vols, Paris: Éditions du Cerf, 1968-73.

Wolters, O.W., Southeast Asia as a Southeast Asian Field of Study, *Indonesia*, 58, (1994): 1-17.

2

Indian Contribution to the Archaeology of Its Neighbours

Pravin Srivastava

Introduction

This paper discusses the support the Government of India through the Archaeological Survey of India (ASI) has extended towards capacity-building, preservation of heritage structures and archaeological investigations in neighbouring countries of the Indian Ocean world, particularly with those that share common heritage traditions with India. The ASI was established in the year 1861 for the survey, exploration and documentation of archaeological and architectural sites. By the early twentieth century, conservation of centrally protected monuments, setting up of museums, and the copying and translation of inscriptions were also added to ASI's mandate.

After Indian Independence in 1947, the ASI has continued its responsibility of explorations and excavations of ancient sites and archaeological remains, documentation of religious and secular buildings, conservation and maintenance of monuments and sites, scientific preservation of antiquities and monuments and epigraphic research. It maintains nearly 3700 monuments and archaeological sites in India. It has also extended its efforts to countries outside India. Important among these are explorations

Fig. 2.1. Before and after conservation at Vat Phou Temple in Laos.

and excavations conducted by ASI in Egypt, Nepal and Bahrain; chemical preservation of paintings in Bhutan; establishment of a museum in Angola; structural conservation of Ta Prohm Temple in Cambodia and Vat Phou Temple in Lao PDR (Figs. 2.1–2.2), structural conservation and chemical preservation at Bamiyan in Afghanistan, Angkor Wat Temple in Cambodia (Fig. 2.3), Ananda Temple in Myanmar (Fig. 2.4) and Thiruketeeswaram Temple in Sri Lanka. The conservation of some other monuments such as My Son Group of Temples in Vietnam and Aapravasi Ghat in Mauritius are likely to be taken up by ASI shortly since the proposals are under

Fig. 2.2. Vat Phou Temple in Laos after conservation.

active consideration of the Ministry of External Affairs.

A History of Collaborative Projects

This section provides a brief overview of collaborative projects undertaken by ASI and respective countries.

Indonesia

In 1948, the Government of Indonesia invited two officers from the ASI, K.R. Srinivasan and C. Sivaramamurti, to prepare a detailed report on the Borobudur Stupa and to suggest measures for conservation of the monument. The problem of safeguarding Borobudur became an international one as soon as the Republic of Indonesia was recognized (1950) and joined the United Nations and UNESCO. The opportunity was seized to take advantage of the latest developments in technology and their application to archaeology, and of UNESCO's ability to mobilize international

Fig. 2.3. Samundra manthan gallery during conservation work.

Fig. 2.4. Ananda Temple at Myanmar after conservation.

skills and technical assistance on behalf of its Member States. In 1955, the Government of Indonesia asked UNESCO to advise on the problem of counteracting stone weathering in Indonesian monuments, and Chandi Borobudur in particular.

Nepal

A Department of Archaeology was set up in Nepal in 1952, shortly after King Tribhuvan opened the country to Indian archaeologists. The then Director-General of ASI, Mr. A. Ghosh, visited the country to provide advice on the organisation of the department. Soon after, Dr. R.V. Joshi undertook archaeological investigations in the Kathmandu valley on a prehistoric site (Joshi 1966; Deo 1968).

The valley has also yielded fine images of numerous Vaishnava and Shaiva deities (incarnations and forms of the gods Vishnu and Shiva) as well as of Surya, Brahma and various forms of Devis (goddesses), made between the fifth and tenth centuries. Starting from the tenth century, the art idioms and conventions of Nepal become increasingly prominent and the icons show unmistakable traits of local physiognomy and facial features, which together with the distinctive art conventions of Nepal tend towards greater stylisation and complexity. From the eleventh century onwards, hundreds of Buddhist deities were conceived and fashioned under the influence of Tantrayana and Vajrayana sects, which gained special popularity in Nepal (*Indian Archaeology – A Review 1963-64*, 100-01). ASI and the Department of Archaeology & Culture of His Majesty's Government, Nepal, carried out an iconographical survey in May-June 1963, which included photo documentation of icons in temples and stray images in the Kathmandu valley.

Under the Aid-Nepal programme, the seventeenth century mural paintings in the palace at Bhaktapur, about 12 kilometres from Kathmandu, were chemically treated and preserved. The paintings were carefully documented by the preparation of outline drawings, black-and-white photographs and colour-transparencies. In the course of the work, two trainees of the Department of Archaeology, HM Government of Nepal were given practical training in the chemical preservation and conservation of mural paintings (*Indian Archaeology – A Review 1965-66*, 108-09).

Bahrain

In another example of collaboration, a team from ASI excavated a complex of burial mounds adjacent to the development of a new township near Hamad town, Bahrain in 1985 (*Indian Archaeology – A Review 1985-86*, 190-02). The building and development of the nearby township made the archaeological work urgent. About seventy graves were excavated and were subdivided into four types. A majority of the graves did not yield any grave goods, but some contained pottery, beads of various materials, steatite circular seals, copper rings, rods and a spearhead. On the basis of pottery and seals, graves of Type II have been dated from 2200 to 2000 BC; Type III from 2000 to 1800 BC; and Type IV from 1800 to 1600 BC. An object of special mention in Grave no. 1757 included a circular Indus seal, placed almost in the centre of the burial chamber. The presence of the Indus seal suggests the movement of goods and a relationship between Bahrain, Mesopotamia and the Indus Valley civilization in antiquity.

Cambodia

In 1980, in response to an appeal by Prince Norodom Sihanouk, a small team from ASI visited Cambodia to report on the damage to the twelfth century temple of Angkor Vat and other monuments (*Indian Archaeology – A Review 1981-82*, 137-38). According to their recommendations three persons from Cambodia were given training in conservation and photography. Some equipment and instruments were also made available to them to start documentation and preliminary work on preservation (Figs. 2.5–2.6). In February 1982 another ASI team went to Cambodia to prepare a

Fig. 2.5. Pediment at Angkor Wat (Before treatment).

Fig. 2.6. Pediment at Angkor Wat (After treatment).

comprehensive project report on the preservation of the temple of Angkor Wat, and as a result conservation work was done for several seasons from 1986 to 1993. The Ministry of External Affairs financed this work through its ITEC programme.

UNESCO declared Angkor a World Heritage Site in December 1992, and Angkor Wat, Ta

Phrom, Prea Khan, Bayon, Beng Mealea and other complexes were recognized as World Heritage Monuments. After an inter-governmental conference in Tokyo in 1993, an International Coordinating Committee (ICC) was established to oversee the restoration work at Angkor. The committee meets several times a year in plenary and technical sessions, and the Khmers themselves are active participants through the establishment of APSARA (Authority for the Protection of the Sites and Administration of the Region of Angkor). The Government of India offered to restore and conserve the Ta Phrom complex, and ASI undertook this challenging task in December 2004.

Nearly three years of extensive documentation, studies and analysis gave the ASI team an insight into the issues involved in the preservation of the temple (Figs. 2.7–2.8). After analyzing the entire monument, the ASI decided

Fig. 2.7. Documentation of 4th gopura, elevation East.

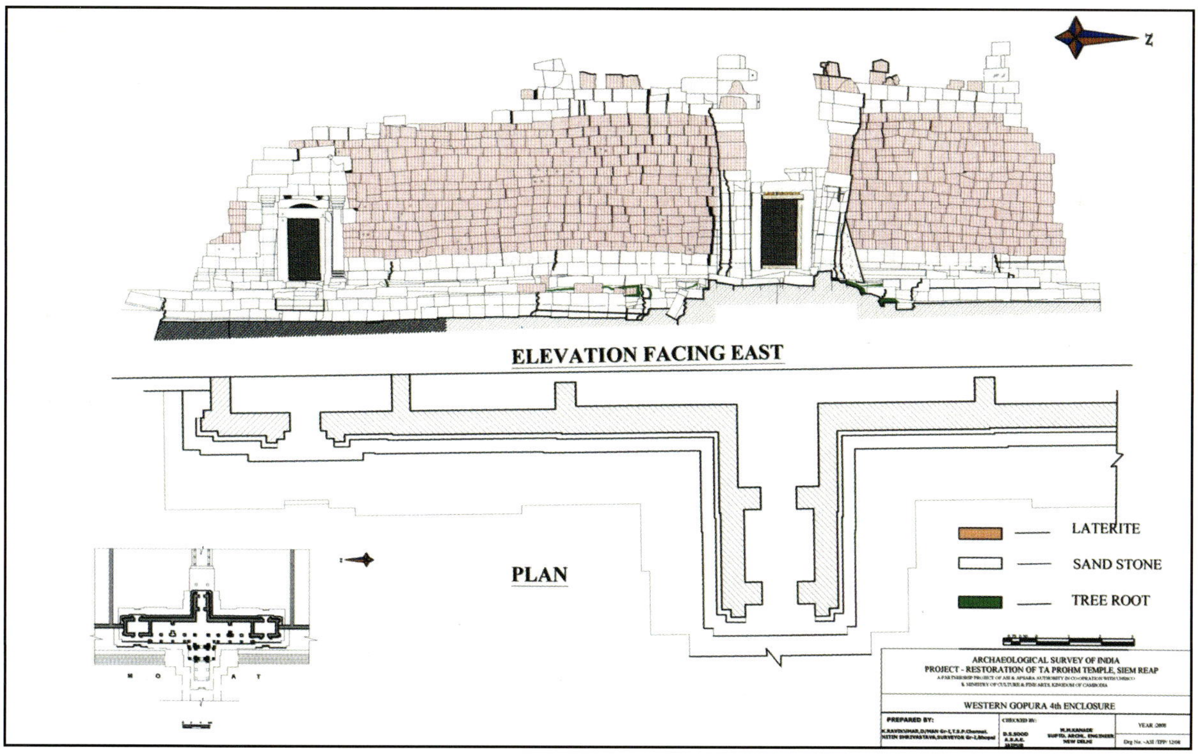

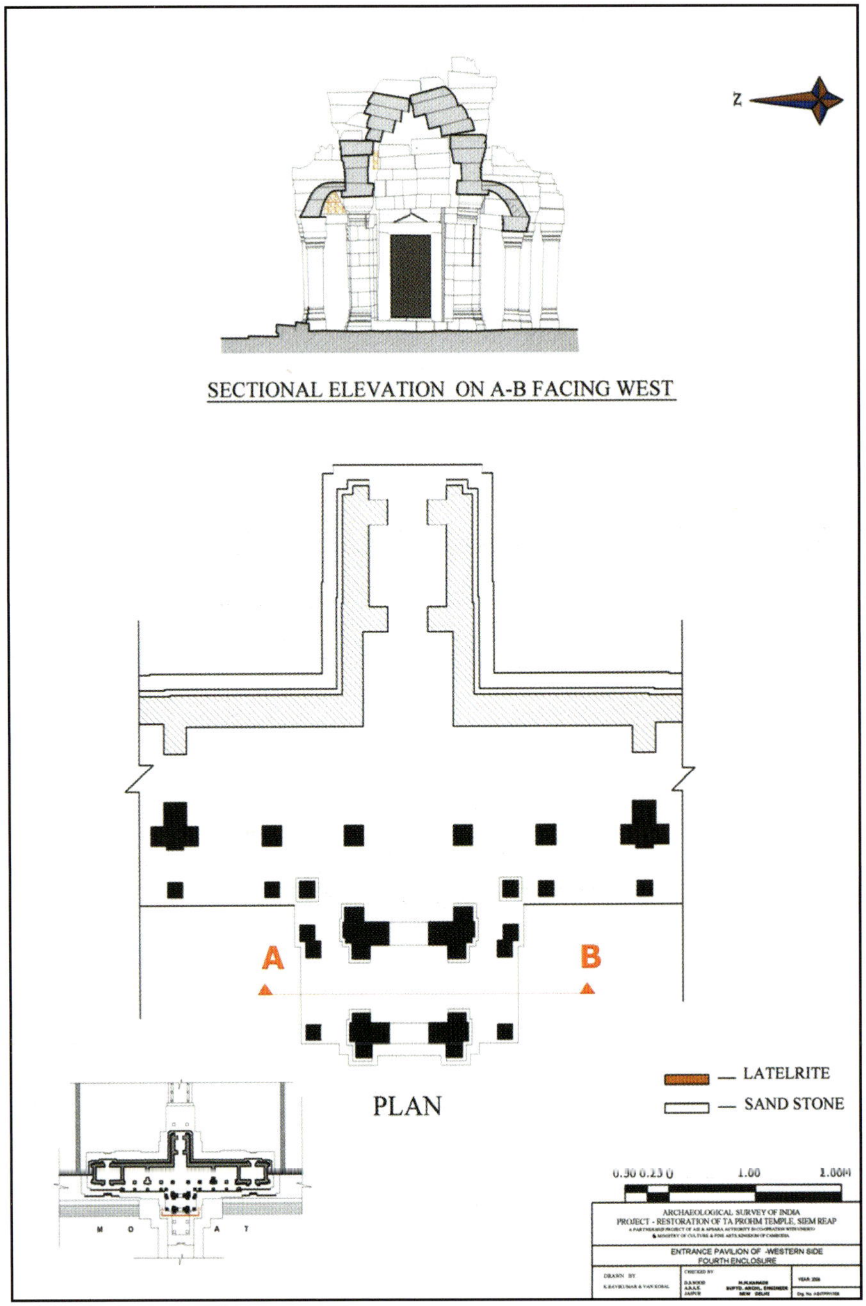

Fig. 2.8. Documentation of 4th gopura, Section.

Fig. 2.9. Wooden Walkway constructed near Hall of Dancers at Ta Phrom to ensure smooth flow of visitors.

that it would restore five structures – the third enclosure gallery on the eastern side of the south wing; the causeway connecting the third and fourth enclosures on the west; part of the Hall of Dancers (Fig. 2.9); the entrance gopura of the fourth enclosure on the western side; and the entrance gate gopura of the fifth enclosure on the west (Fig. 2.10).

An inscription in Sanskrit in Khmer script in the Ta Phrom complex records that a township

BEFORE INTERVENTION

DURING INTERVENTION

WEST ENTRANCE GOPURA 5th ENCLOSURE

Fig. 2.10. Conservation at Ta Phrom temple.

flourished between the fourth and fifth enclosures of the temple. The complex had nineteen Buddhist high priests. The inscription states that it had 500 kilograms each of gold and silver, diamonds weighing 35 kg, and 4,600 pearls. The ASI documented every stone member layer by layer and grid by grid; measured every sandstone block for its length, height and width; and recorded their quality and orientation. The entire hall was photographed bit by bit. Then the dismantling of the floor was done, the soil was treated appropriately and sandstone blocks of the floor and the plinth were reset. The original broken stones of the floors, columns and roof were repaired and joined with appropriate material and threaded with steel pins. It was ensured that all architectural members achieved the desired structural strength before they were reassembled. The restoration work began in 2007, and due to the project's multidisciplinary nature, took support from the Forest Research Institute (FRI), Dehradun; Water and Power Consultancy Service Limited (WAPCOS), New Delhi; and the Indian Institute of Technology, Madras.

Conclusion

This paper highlights the Archaeological Survey of India's explorations and initiatives in the surrounding countries of the Indian Ocean. Project 'Mausam,' a new project by the Ministry of Culture, Government of India, will allow for new avenues of cooperation and collaboration in archaeological research and heritage conservation efforts between India and its neighbours. These capacity-building initiatives will be further strengthened once the proposed UNESCO Category-II Centre for World Heritage proposed by India is established by ASI. The resources of Indian national institutions for such initiatives are well-recognized by UNESCO, and India is keen to be at the forefront of this proposal. The Centres for Natural and Cultural Heritage are a much awaited initiative for capacity-building of World Heritage in the Asia Region.

References

Indian Archaeology – A Review 1963-64, (1967), A. Ghosh (ed.), New Delhi: Archaeological Survey of India.

Indian Archaeology – A Review 1965-66, (1973), A. Ghosh (ed.), New Delhi: Archaeological Survey of India.

Indian Archaeology – A Review 1981-82, (1983), Debala Mitra (ed.), New Delhi: Archaeological Survey of India.

Indian Archaeology – A Review 1985-86, (1990), J.P. Joshi (ed.), New Delhi: Archaeological Survey of India.

Deo, S.B., *Archaeological Investigations in the Nepal Terai 1964*, Kathmandu: Department of Archaeology, 1968.

Joshi, R.V., Prehistoric Exploration in the Katmandu Valley, Nepal, *Ancient India*, 22, (1966): 75-82.

3

The Archaeology of Kachchh in Gujarat: Defining Cultural Landscapes

Yaduvir Singh Rawat

"The Rann of Kutch is a vast, lonely desert, almost impossible to cross. Yet, some people do cross it for reasons of their own...."

(Daruwala and Abdulla 2011)

These lines by India's celebrated poet and short story writer graphically portray the isolation often associated with Kachchh, which is however belied by the archaeological data and the tremendous antiquity of the region dating to the prehistoric period. The island of Kachchh derives its name from its unique geomorphological form in the shape of a tortoise, which is locally called as 'Kachbo' in Gujarati or 'Kachua' in Hindi. It is not only a distinctive geographic phenomenon, but more importantly the region is well-known for its unrivalled textiles with exquisite embroidery and mirror-work. Much of the Rann consists of the world's largest salt desert, measuring around 10,000 square kilometres. What makes this expanse extraordinary is that the salt desert is underwater during the monsoon season from June to September. Geo-archaeological studies have shown that from seven thousand to almost a thousand years ago, the Rann was an extension of the Arabian Sea and received waters and sediments from the Himalayan rivers (Merh 2011, 11-12).

Kachchh may be classified into four distinct physiological zones: The Great Rann in the north and the Little Rann in the east; in the centre, the plains are interspersed with various hills like Katrol, Wagad etc; the Banni plains are marked by the grassland area sandwiched between the Great Rann in the north and Mainland Kachchh in the south; while the coastal zone includes the areas from Kori creek in the north down to the south till the extreme end of the Gulf of Kachchh, adjacent to the Little Rann in the east.

The beginnings of archaeology in Kachchh date to 1876 when James Burgess of the Archaeological Survey of India undertook a systematic survey of the monuments of Kachchh and published a *Report on the Antiquities of Kathiawad and Kutch* (1876). This was followed in 1879 by a report on the archaeological remains by D.P. Khakhar, the then Educational Inspector. In the 1960s, archaeologists from several institutions, such as Deccan College, Pune; MS University, Vadodara; Gujarat State Department of Archaeology and the Archaeological Survey of India undertook intensive survey and excavations in the region and discovered a large number of sites dating to the third-second millennium BCE Harappan period.

The Bronze Age

The beginnings of settlement in the region date to the Bronze Age civilization of South Asia, characterized by urban centres and a standardized material culture. Several archaeological excavations in Gujarat over the last five decades have lead to the discovery of over 550 Harappan-period sites, which have been classified as cities, towns and villages. The largest of these in Gujarat is the 47 hectare quadrangular city of Dholavira, which lay between two seasonal streams, the Mansar in the north and Manhar in the south. Only a few sites of Saurashtra have shown evidence of fortification, whereas all the sites in Kachchh, big or small, have the distinct feature of being fortified. Most of the sites are situated on the banks of rivers or small rivulets, but the location of a few sites show that they were strategically planned in order to utilize marine resources.

Of the four areas of Kachchh, Harappan sites are mainly seen in and around the Great Rann, the Little Rann and the coastal area near Gulf of Kachchh. About forty-four Harappan or Harappan-affined sites have been located so far along the Gujarat coast. Thirty of these belong to the Urban and the rest to the Late or Post-Urban

Fig. 3.1. Khirsara Harappan site showing reuse of archeological material for present worship.

period. In terms of coastal locations, nineteen are in Kachchh (including the Rann) and twenty-five in Saurashtra and the mainland. Only nine fortified settlements have been recorded so far. Except Lothal, they are mainly on the coast of the Gulf of Kachchh or the Rann (Rawat 2014).

The two major sites of Dholavira and Juni Kuran are situated in the islands of the Great Rann, namely, the Khadir and the Pascham. Pabumath is also situated in Great Rann area, twenty kilometres south of Dholavira. The sites of Khirsara (Fig. 3.1), Desalpur, Kotada Bhadli are

Fig. 3.2. A bird's eye view of Kanmer from south.

located near the north-western edge of Great Rann, more towards the coastal margin of Kachchh. Sites like Shikarpur, Kanmer (Fig. 3.2) and the recently explored Navinal lie near the Gulf of Kachchh, while Surkotada, a major fortified site (Fig. 3.3) is situated near the Little Rann of Kachchh. Thus the distribution pattern of sites discovered so far indicate Harappan occupation in the areas of the Great Rann, the Little Rann and the coastal part near the Gulf of Kachchh.

The site of Dholavira, located in Khadir island of the Rann of Kachchh, is known for its urban planning and water management systems

Fig. 3.3. Fortification wall at Surkotada.

as early as 3000 BCE to 1800 BCE. In the words of the excavator: "The site is remarkable for its exquisite planning, monumental structures, aesthetic architecture, efficient water harvesting system and funerary architecture" (Bisht 1991, 1997). These unique features of the site have been acknowledged by its nomination to the Tentative List of UNESCO's World Heritage Sites.

A cemetery with a variety of funerary structures was found around a large ancient reservoir situated to the west of the ancient city. The most remarkable sepulchral structure type was in the form of large tumuli. These circular spoke-wheel type plans have a central chamber which was opened and reused as and when required. Initially, these hemispherical structures were made of mud brick, but in subsequent phases, stone was also used. Among other significant findings at the site is an inscription composed of ten large-sized signs in the Indus script. It has been identified as a signboard that may have been once hung on the façade of the north gate of the citadel. The site has also provided evidence of industrial activities. Workshops for manufacture of beads, shell objects, lapidary, etc., have been excavated.

Saran, on the shore of the Great Rann of Kachchh, is about three and a half kilometres north of Dholavira and seems to be a small Harappan port catering to the needs of the ancient metropolis. The site is located on the left bank of a rivulet, while on the flat top of the outcrop are the ruins of a large rectangular building oriented east-west. This building may have been a warehouse for the temporary storage of goods.

Kuntasi, on the southern shore of the Gulf of Kachchh, stands on the right bank of a seasonal river named Phulki in Rajkot district. The Gulf is about five kilometres from the site and Navlakhi, a non-major port, is situated further north-west into the Gulf, about eight kilometres away, though the site may have been on the coast in the Harappan period. Excavations revealed structures dated to the Harappan and Late Harappan periods around an oblong open area. The excavator has identified a stone built wharf along the western margin of the site (Dhavalikar 2011, 261-62). A few of the interesting structures along the riverfront include a ramp leading to the river, a watchtower and a platform. The ramp was located at the south-eastern corner of the settlement between the eastern and the southern arms of the fortification. It was 4.10 m wide and 9.50 m long and was built of boulders set in mud mortar with large flat stones along the edge. According to the excavator, it might have provided for facilitating the movement of goods from within the fortified area to the river.

Sites such as Nageshwar, Shikarpur, Bagasra have revealed presence of raw materials. The site of Nageshwar, for example, was littered with heaps of cut and uncut shells (*Turbinella pyrum*) and a large quantity of wasters (Dhavalikar 2011, 263). The ancient site at Bagasra in Maliya taluka of Rajkot District is located on the south-eastern shore of Gulf of Kachchh. Excavations at the site revealed typical Harappan steatite seals, terracotta sealings and many other objects made of a variety of stone, shell, bone, metal and clay. Then there are sites like Surkotda, Kanmer, Kotada Bhadli (Fig. 3.4) and Desalpur which

Fig. 3.4. Rural Harappan site of Kotada Bhadli.

seem to have evolved due to their geographical locations, whereas sites like Juni Kuran (Fig. 3.5), Dholavira, Khirsara, Lothal were known for craft manufacturing activities.

Several sites in Kachchh show evidence of settlement both in Harappan and Early Historic periods. These include sites such as Kerasi, two kilometres west of Gedi, which is considered to be one of the oldest towns in Kachchh (*Indian Archaeology – A Review 1965-66*, 14); Lakhpat located at the mouth of the Kori creek and surrounded by eighteenth century fort walls

(Fig. 3.6); Netra Khirasara twenty seven kilometres north-west of Nakhtarana (*Indian Archaeology – A Review 1976-77*, 38); Kotada located north of Anjar (*Indian Archaeology – A Review 1965-66*, 16) and so on. There are still several gaps in our understanding of the transition to the historical period, but architectural remains, inscriptions and literary sources have helped in fleshing out the historical narrative.

The Historical Period

The western Kshatrapas or Satraps who ruled in Saurashtra and Malwa in the early centuries of the Common Era are largely known through their

Fig. 3.5. Harappan site of Junikuran.

Fig. 3.6. Lakhpat Pir Ghaus Mohammed tomb.

Fig. 3.7. Aina Mahal at Bhuj.

inscriptions and coinage. In contrast to many of their contemporaries in central and peninsular India, the Kshatrapas used Greek legends on their coinage (Bhandare 2006). Six families of the Kshtrapas are known to have ruled over a region extending from the north-western part of the subcontinent to Gujarat. Kachchh has yielded nine of a total of thirty stone inscriptions of the Kshatrapa dynasty known from western India. Six of the epigraphs, the earliest of these being that of

Chastana dated to 89 CE, were recovered from the village of Andhau in Kachchh district in the nineteenth century. These inscriptions, written in the Brahmi script using the Sanskrit language mixed with Prakrit, are now kept in the museum at Bhuj which was established in 1877 (Figs. 3.7–3.8). The objective of all the nine inscriptions is to honour the memory of a deceased ancestor and to record the setting up of funerary monuments (Fig. 3.9).

The inscriptions were coeval with Buddhist caves, which were excavated in the coastal regions of Gujarat, dating from the second century BCE to the sixth century CE. Rock-cut caves are known from Kateshwar and five from Siyot in Lakhpat taluka in the extreme north-west of Kachchh, and bronze images of the Buddha have also been found datable from fourth to seventh centuries CE. Exploration at the site of Nani Rayan, a small village on the banks of the river Rukmavati, which meets the Arabian Sea at the port of Mandvi four kilometres away, has provided a rich haul of valuable archaeological material including etched carnelian beads, shell bangles, mould-made and stamped pottery and coins. These suggest occupation of Nani Rayan from fourth and third centuries BCE onward, although excavation work has yet to be undertaken at the site (Vasa 2011, 281-96). The temple of Dada Dhoramnath at the site is a six metre-high fort-like structure, which provides a vantage point for observing the entire length of the river until it meets the sea.

Bhadresvara was an early site on the coast of Kachchh in Gujarat. It was also the site of a twelfth century Jain temple thirty-two kilometres from Mundra on the north coast of the Gulf of Kachchh. An inscription refers to it as a *velakula* or harbour (Burgess, 1876, 206-07). Burgess also reported finding a hero stone or *paliya* from the site with a ship carved on it, indicating that it was set up in memory of a person who lost his life at sea (Burgess 1876, 205). Bhadresvara is at present a small village and a site of pilgrimage, but in ancient times it was a fortified coastal centre. The Sanskrit text *Jagaducarita* records that the town was a city-state run in the eleventh and twelfth century by a council of Jain merchants under the suzerainty of the Chaulukyas of Gujarat. Jagadu is said to have built a mosque here for the Ismaili sect and the local Muslim community with the permission of the Jain Council, but the most notable structure is the shrine of Ibrahim dated on the basis of an *in situ* inscription to 1159-1160 CE, i.e. nearly half a century earlier than the Islamic monuments at Delhi or Ajmer. In Bhadresvara and at several other sites in Gujarat such as Cambay, Somnath and Patan, there are a number of tombstones dated between mid-twelfth and early thirteenth centuries CE. Many of the architectural features at Bhadresvara are also found in a mosque built by early settlers at Junagadh in Saurashtra, where an inscription records that the chief merchant and ship-owner, Abu'l-Qasim bin 'Ali al-Idhaji built the mosque in 685 AH/1286-87 CE.

Thus the continued maritime linkages of Kachchh from prehistory to the historical period

Fig. 3.8. Fortifications at Bhuj.

Fig. 3.9. Paliya or memorial stones.

are evident. In the next section we shift the discussion to present an overview of the seafaring traditions of the region.

Coastal Settlements, and Traditions of Boat-building and Sailing

Archaeological investigations in western India have provided information on several long-lasting coastal settlements. A consideration of the *longue durée* at Mandvi, on the estuary of the Rukmavati River at the entrance to the Gulf of Kachchh, is appropriate for this article. Mandvi was officially founded as a port town by Khengarji, the king of Kachchh, in 1574. The first temple to be built there was the Sundarwar temple, followed by the Jama Masjid in 1603, the Lakshminarayan Temple in 1607, the Kajivali Mosque in 1608 and the Rameshwar Temple in 1627. For all these to have been built within the first fifty years of the town's existence is a clear indicator of its importance to the kingdom. Indeed, at its peak, Mandvi's wealth easily surpassed that of the capital at Bhuj. It was only after ships grew too large for its harbour and began to prefer Mumbai that Mandvi's importance as a port began to fade.

Mandvi has been known as a port town with links to both Oman and the East African coast since archaeological explorations were conducted there in the mid-19th century. In addition to a range of ceramics, important finds included local and regional coins, as well as a Byzantium Solidus of Heraclius dated to 638 CE and an Arab Umayyad dinar of 716 CE (Vasa 1990). Writing in 1836, Alexander Burnes described maritime activities at Mandvi as follows:

> The principal seaport of Kutch is Mandavee, which stands in lat. 22° 51'N and long. 69° 34'E close to the Gulf. It has no fewer than 250 vessels belonging to it, and boasts a population of 50,000 souls, which is about one-eighth of that of the whole province of Kutch. It is an open roadstead with a creek. From Mandavee a maritime communication is kept up with Zanguebar and the whole east coast of Africa, with the Red Sea and Arabia and with the Persian Gulf, Mekrom and Sinde and with India as far as Ceylon. The vessels used in this extensive commerce vary in size from 100 to 800 candies or from 25 to 200 tons. They carry a large lateen sail, have two masts and are never decked (Burnes 1836).

Ethnographic data indicates that the coastal settlements participated in trade with other centres further south and also across the Ocean, though each port specialized in a particular route. Mandvi, Porbandar and Veraval traded with East Africa; and Porbandar and Veraval with South Arabia, Southeast Asia and the Persian Gulf. Thus route specialization is an important aspect of seafaring activity that has far-reaching implications for a study of the past as well (Orton 2001, 100-101). Another critical factor is the sailing season, which in Gujarat comes to an end in June, after which the monsoon winds become too dangerous until end-July.

The first century CE Greek text, the *Periplus Maris Erythraei,* perhaps provides the first detailed description of local boats in the Indian Ocean in the early centuries CE. It also refers to several types of port settlements from the East African coast to the west coast of India. In the context of Gujarat, the *Periplus* refers to Syrastrene or Surashtra, and Eirinon or the Rann of Kutch, beyond which lies Barake or the Gulf of Kutch (Section 40). This is a dangerous Gulf to navigate for, "not only are the waves there very big and oppressive, but the sea is choppy and turbid, with eddies and violent whirlpools." (Section 40). After this the author mentions the

Gulf of Barygaza, which is presently identified with the Gulf of Cambay (Section 41). One aspect that is missing from the *Periplus* is any reference to the local communities.

In this respect, ethnographic data shows the participation of sailing communities across Gujarat. In fact, Kachchh is still renowned for its traditions of sailing and seafaring, and cultural memory associates a sailor from the Kharva community of Kachchh with navigating the Portuguese explorer Vasco da Gama (1460-1524) to India. Inhabiting the villages of Mandvi, Mundra, Jamnagar, Beyt, Jam Salaaya, Okha and so on, the Kharvas continue to be involved with ship-building and sailing on sea-going vessels. Successful Kharvas become ship owners and captains or *nakhodas* (Orton 2001).

The present communities engage in a variety of rituals and beliefs associated with the sea. There is evidence of rituals performed at each stage of construction of the water-craft which are compiled in a book titled *Nauka Navghatan Pujanam* or 'Worship for New Ship Construction'. Communities linked to coastal temples dedicate to a range of deities and often donate regularly for maintenance as well as for performance of rituals. Another feature in the religious landscape is the memorial stone or *paliyar* set up in memory of those who lost their life at sea. It is also significant that these temple structures often double as markers to identify the coasts and are often associated with local legends of saviours at sea. Thus, religious architecture fulfils both religious and navigational purposes and this was important in an earlier period also.

The article has examined the history of Kachchh often referred to as an isolated area in western India and established its participation in the wider maritime network. A combination of prehistoric, historic and ethnographic evidence points to the importance of sea-faring trade and the enormous impact of the sea in life in Kachchh, from antiquity to the present. The overall picture that emerges is that most of the sites of the Gujarat region, and those located south of the Great Rann (Fig. 3.10), worked as partners.

Geological investigations in the Rann of Kachchh have shown that the Little Rann had 4 m deep water until 2000 years ago. The excavations at Kanmer have provided evidence that the entire Gulf of Kachchh and the Rann were navigable in the Bronze Age and connected to the Indus region in the north and Gujarat in the south through waterways. The location of Harappan sites on both coasts of the Gulf further supports this hypothesis and suggests that both small and large settlements participated in exchange networks

Fig. 3.10. Karim Shahi in the centre of the Great Rann of Kachchh.

though their ambit may have been different. It is this focus on geological and archaeological investigations that make a study of the Kachchh region fascinating for Project Mausam.

References

Bhandare, Shailendra, A Tale of Two Dynasties: The Kshaharatas and the Satavahanas in Deccan, in Himanshu Prabha Ray (ed.), *Coins in India: Power and Communication; Marg,* Volume 57, 3, Mumbai: Marg Publications, 2006.

Bisht, Ravi S., Dholavira: A New Horizon of the Indus Civilization, *Puratattva*, 20 (1991): 71-82.

Bisht, Ravi S., Dholavira Excavations: 1990-94, in J.P. Joshi (ed.), *Facets of Indian Civilization: Recent Perspectives*, pp. 107-120, New Delhi: Aryan Books International, 1997.

Burgess, James, *Report on the Antiquities of Kathiawad and Kachchh*, Archaeological Survey of Western India, London: W.H. Allen & Co, 1876.

Burnes, Alexander, On the Maritime Communications of India as Carried on by Natives Particularly from Kutch at the Mouth of the Indus, *Journal of the Royal Geographical Society of London*, VI (1836).

Daruwalla, Keki N. and V. Abdulla, *Love Across the Salt Desert*, New Delhi: Penguin Books India, 2011.

Dhavalikar, M.K., Core and Periphery: Harappans in Gujarat, in Lotika Varadarajan (ed.), *Gujarat and the Sea,* pp. 253-64, Vadodara: Darshak Itihas Nidhi, 2011.

Orton, Nancy Pinto, Sea-Going Trade in Early Historic Gujarat (c. 100 BC to AD 500), Unpublished Ph.D. diss., University of Pennsylvania, 2001.

Rawat, Yaduvir S., Possible Port Towns of the Harappans, Paper presented at the Project Mausam Lecture at India International Centre, New Delhi, India, April 25, 2014.

Merh, Sukumar S., Changing Land-Sea Relationship in the Ranns of Kachchh: A Geo-archaeological Perspective, in Lotika Varadarajan (ed.), *Gujarat and the Sea,* pp. 11-32, Vadodara: Darshak Itihas Nidhi, 2011.

Vasa, P.N., Find of a Late Byzantine Solidus and Arab Umayyad Dinara from Kutch, *Numismatic Digest* 14 (1990): 30-33.

Vasa, Pulin, Nani Rayan in Kachchh: Archaeological Evidences of Shipping and Trade in Ancient India, in Lotika Varadarajan (ed.), *Gujarat and the Sea,* pp. 281-96, Vadodara: Darshak Itihas Nidhi, 2011.

4

Re-examining 'Fringes' in Prehistory: Arabian Coastal Landscapes

Akshyeta Suryanarayan

Introduction

Archaeological and historical research has long been preoccupied with the great riverine civilizations of Egypt, Mesopotamia, the Indus and China, with an asymmetric interest in the history of the sea and the surrounding regions of Asia. This narrow preoccupation has been rooted in discourses framed by notions of 'centres' and 'peripheries' in antiquity, with the paucity of textual sources from these so-called 'fringe areas' in Asia contributing heavily to these binary divisions of ancient societies. Ideas of "grand, literate Civilizations" versus the "less 'civilized', 'illiterate' societies" on their borders have prevailed in scholarship, grossly oversimplifying the diversity of social organisation and interactions in the past (Potts 1999).

In recent years, however, there has been a marked effort to move away from simplistic and reductionist views of antiquity. 'Civilizations' are coming to be understood through the diversity of their social organization and cooperation, and formative processes as well as their 'achievements' (Cleuziou and Tosi, 2007). The present paper focuses on how the rapid progress of archaeological investigation in the present-day

United Arab Emirates (UAE) and the Sultanate of Oman has altered our understanding of ancient Arabia, long considered a 'peripheral' zone and unworthy of scholarly attention (Potts 1999). Highlighting the contribution of recent archaeological field surveys and excavations in the UAE and Sultanate of Oman, this paper also takes the opportunity to re-examine another area of research long exiled to the 'fringes' of archaeological and historical scholarship: that is, coastal settlements and landscapes. The paper calls for the holistic examination of coastal sites and urgent need for their care, listing challenges to their preservation.

The paper next discusses Tell Abraq, a site in the UAE on the coast of the Arabian Gulf. It seeks to highlight Tell Abraq's autonomous coastal nature, which can be used as an analogy for other coastal sites in South Eastern Arabia. It also explains the role it and other coastal settlements played in facilitating interactions between foreign, coastal and inland areas in Southeastern Arabia in the mid-third millennium BCE. Finally, the paper calls attention to the value of archaeological fieldwork at coastal sites, and how its use, like in South East Arabia, will be hugely beneficial in re-defining narratives and documenting the rich coastal heritage of other Indian Ocean world countries. Project 'Mausam', a new initiative by the Ministry of Culture, Government of India could help bring these marginalized coastal sites into the forefront of archaeological research and heritage preservation.

Archaeology in Southeastern Arabia

The archaeological exploration of Southeastern Arabia did not start in earnest until the late 1950s, largely due to notions in scholarship that viewed it as an area at the fringes of developments in ancient history (Magee 2014, 1). It was primarily the search for oil which served as a catalyst for exploration in this area and precipitated the rise of archaeological investigation. Beginning in 1958, American oilman Wendell Phillips, father of the American Foundation for the Study of Man, undertook a short season of excavation at Sohar, in Oman. In the same year, Temple Hillyard, whose emic knowledge resulted from working for British Petroleum in Abu Dhabi, contracted with two Danish archaeologists visiting from Bahrain to examine a number of graves he had discovered (Potts 1999). These excavations resulted in the discovery of a Bronze Age culture that was previously unknown to the world, which generated new interest among scholars and researchers of the ancient Near East (Magee 2014, 88). However, research in South East

Fig. 4.1. Coastline of Abu Dhabi from the 1960's.

Arabia remained sporadic through the 1960s (Fig. 4.1), until political conditions across the region changed dramatically in the 1970s. The creation of the United Arab Emirates in conjunction with the reign of Sultan Qaboos in the Sultanate of Oman enabled dozens of surveys and excavations in the area, contributing to our understanding of the prehistory that has dramatically changed in a surprisingly short period of forty years (Potts 1999).

Conceptualizing Coastal Landscapes

Coastal settlements have been traditionally viewed as nodes embedded within trade networks, liminal spaces that facilitate the movement of goods from one place to another. They are popularly imagined as harbour-towns where ships loaded or unloaded cargo (seen 'from the foreign' or 'for the foreign') and consequently are often plotted on maps in a manner to suggest relationships to other ports 'just like them'. Another problem with this tradition is that maritime and terrestrial interactions are rarely considered in tandem, but instead are mapped over different geographies and considered in different contexts (Doonan 2004). It is often forgotten that a range of interdependent or mutually supportive land-and sea-based adaptations exist at coastal areas which allow for connectivity and exchange between lands beyond the sea and the inland (Figs. 4.2–4.3).

Similarly, international trade and exchange, although important, often overshadow the equally significant structures, systems, and processes occurring at coastal settlements themselves, which are not always dependent on an international network. Popular notions of the dependence of coastal settlements on outside influences is likely because the human waterfront displays a "unique openness to impulses and impressions from the outside" (Westerdahl 1992, 6). Archaeologists have, in recent years, called for a theoretical reorientation away from over-studied land-based narratives that marginalize the complex processes, exchanges, and interactions occurring at coastlines and seaways (Bailey 2004, Westerdahl 1992). The diversity of economic, political, social processes inside each coastal settlement and its environs is as important as external processes (such as long-distance trade or colonization) in shaping the overall organization of the network.

One way to rectify this attitude is to approach coastal settlements and communities that lived at the edge of water holistically; it should be recognized that the coastal cultural landscape signifies a combination of "*human utilization (economy) of maritime space by boat: settlement, fishing, hunting, shipping and its attendant subcultures,* such as pilotage, lighthouse and seamark maintenance" (Westerdahl 1992, 5, emphasis original) as well as terrestrial aspects of 'inland seaways'. Additionally, coastal settlements may not necessarily be involved in direct trade, but could be important navigational markers or refueling points for boats. All of these elements need to be considered when discussing *coast-scapes,* because the complementarity of resources between different parts of the coastline, coast and

4.2

4.3

Fig. 4.2–4.3. Interior desert near Mlieha, Sharjah and mangrove at Kalba, on the eastern shore of the UAE.

interior, and coast and offshore islands, further enhances the possibility of social and cultural links and the dispersal and diffusion of people and ideas (Fig. 4.4).

The Value of Survey and Fieldwork in the Understanding of Coastal Landscapes

How does one imagine and reconstruct the coastal landscapes in antiquity? It is here the role of intensive field survey and archaeological excavation is paramount. Field survey, when part of research design, enables the systematic examination of surface deposits, which can then prompt excavation when an area is identified as pertaining to the research question. Once these areas are identified, controlled and methodological excavations reveal a wealth of information about not only the material assemblages of sites, but also allow for a comprehensive chronological and contextual reconstruction of the development of the site and surrounding landscape. Additionally, important information concerning the ancient environment and subsistence strategies can also be collected and then interpreted through geoarchaeological, zooarchaeological and palaeobotanical analysis. Even though the nature of the archaeological record is inherently fragmentary and poor preservation of remains or later occupation of

Fig. 4.4. Dhow boats and buildings by the shore of Dubai.

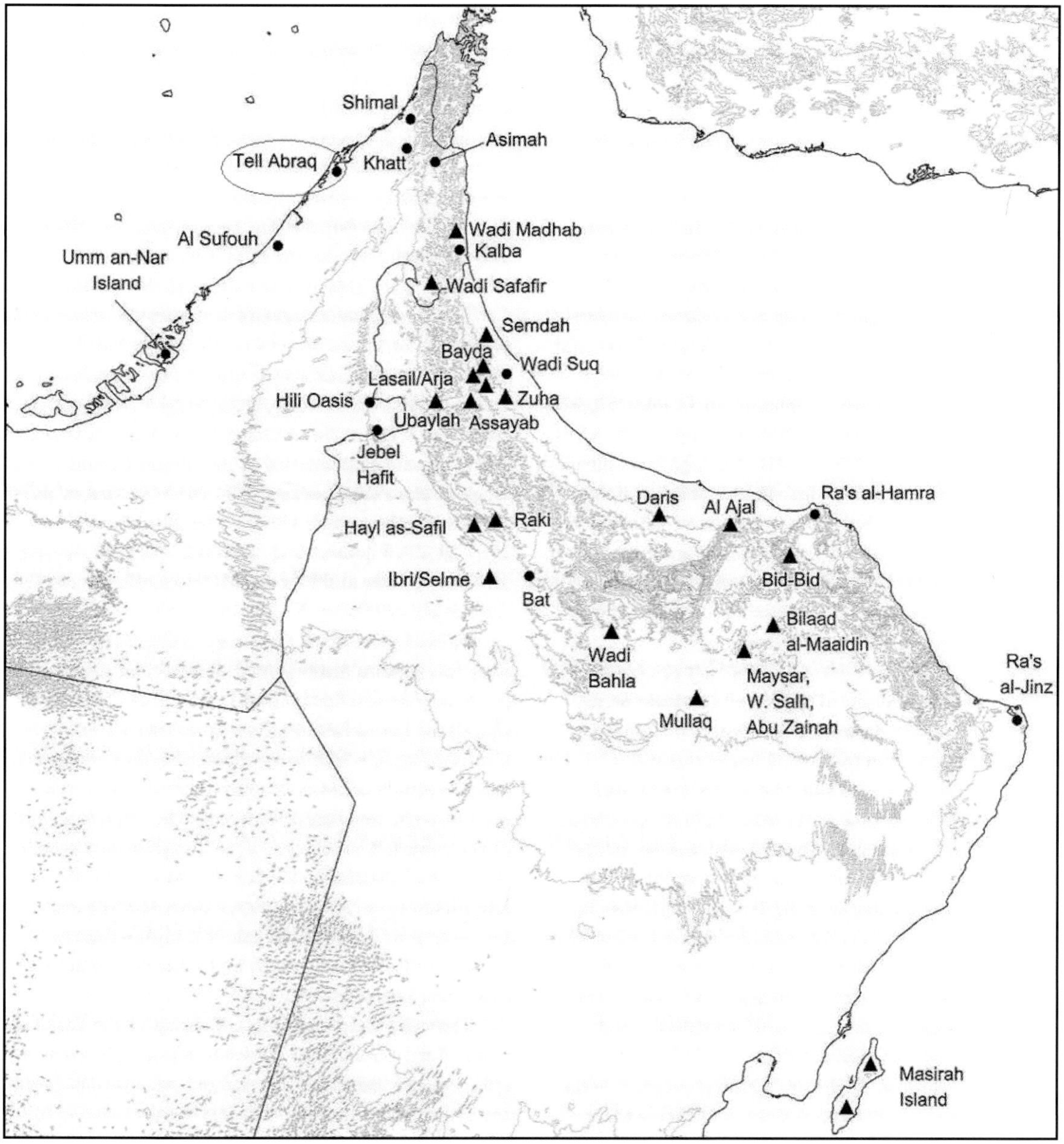

Fig. 4.5. Map of South Eastern Arabia showing third-millennium sites (circles) and copper deposits (triangles). Tell Abraq is circled in red.

sites can be confounding, archaeological data discovered in their stratigraphic context enable a rich reconstruction of the past.

The archaeology and survey of coastal landscapes, however, is fraught with several challenges. Coastal regions are dynamic and highly susceptible to the destructive forces of a wide variety of natural and cultural processes (e.g., tectonic instability, tsunamis, volcanism, attrition, wave and tidal action, sea level rise, storm events, near-shore development, offshore dredging, and coral or sand mining) that threaten the global coastal archaeological record (Rick and Fitzpatrick 2012, 135). These processes cause extensive damage to both terrestrial and submerged archaeological sites; in many cases, catastrophic events may completely destroy evidence for past human occupation. Sea level rise, exacerbated by climate change, is a particularly prominent threat that will erode or destroy a massive number of coastal archaeological sites in the coming decades (Rick and Fitzpatrick 2012, 136). These threats exist in part because many countries lack sufficient laws to protect archaeological sites, particularly in coastal areas where development is extremely desirable, say, for tourism. Archaeologists must work quickly to survey and record the wide array of prehistoric settlements in these regions before they are disturbed or destroyed.

Case Study: Tell Abraq in the Arabian Coastal Landscape

Tell Abraq

The site of Tell Abraq is situated on the borders of the present-day Emirates of Sharjah and Umm al-Quwain in the United Arab Emirates (Fig. 4.5). It is a multi-period site that revealed the first continuously occupied sequence from the third millennium BCE through the Iron Age in Southeastern Arabia, with some remains from the late pre-Islamic periods.

Today, the site is several kilometers away from the coast, but in the third and second millennia BCE it was probably about less than 400m from the sea (Potts 1990a, 236), evidenced by the *sabkha* (salt marsh) that extends over a large part of Umm al-Quwain, which was once a lagoon with mangroves. Thus, Tell Abraq should be considered a coastal site, and can be considered a prominent zone for the interaction of a diverse group of peoples and exchange of goods, given the large amount of foreign goods unearthed (Potts 1999, 27). With well-preserved architectural remains, a long stratigraphic sequence, and an array of material and paleoenvironmental data as well as information about subsistence and settlement patterns, it is one of the most important sites in Southeastern

Fig. 4.6. A view of the mound of Tell Abraq from the south, on an unusually stormy day. Excavations were conducted by the University of Copenhagen and then the the University of Sydney from 1989 to 1998, and are continuing as part of a project by Bryn Mawr College.

Arabia (Potts 1990b). The focus of this paper is on Tell Abraq in the mid- to late third millennium BCE, although the patterns that are evident should be considered as reflective of broader, systemic processes that define this period and others, as Magee and Carter (1999) observe for the late second millennium BCE.

One of the prominent architectural features visible at Tell Abraq is its central fortification system (Fig. 4.6). Potts (1999, 2012) has argued that the tower was undoubtedly the locus of power, on regional, economic, political, and social levels. Examples of such buildings, commonly referred to as 'towers' (Frifelt 1976), have been excavated in many parts of Oman and the United Arab Emirates, from Maysar in the Sharqiyah, to Bidya in the southern Emirates (see Frifelt 1976; Potts 1999). These towers, as well as large communal tombs, dotted the Southeast Arabian landscape in the mid- to late third millennium BCE. One of the largest-known examples of a tower is present at Tell Abraq (Fig. 4.7), and a large communal tomb belonging to the same period, was discovered close to the tower. Excavations have revealed a number of occupation levels with postholes adjoining the tower. One can then picture a large, built-up settlement, with the tower of mudbrick and stone at the centre, surrounded by structures made of palm-fronds that did not survive in the archaeological record.

Fig. 4.7. The remains of the third millennium BCE tower at Tell Abraq.

Potts compares the third-millennium towers to the 15th-century defensive Martello Towers in Corsica, which are defined by an upper surface from which cannons could be fired, and walls thick enough so as to withstand almost any kind of bombardment (2012, 49). While it would be unwise to make any conclusions about the necessity of a defensive structure at the site, these third millennium towers appear to be similar in their general conception. It is not hard to imagine that the tower at Tell Abraq, as well as its large fortification wall and surrounding structures, were visible landmarks from the waters of the Arabian Gulf, possibly guiding wind-powered ships to their destination, and serving as markers in the surrounding landscape.

The Foreign Objects at Tell Abraq

A wide variety of finds from Tell Abraq point to links with sites in Mesopotamia, southwestern

Iran, southeastern Iran, Bahrain, and the Indus Valley (Potts 1993). The tomb at Tell Abraq revealed an array of personal items including necklaces with beads made from various materials, such as shell, bone, frit, carnelian, lapis lazuli, jasper, and agate, which range geographically from Gujarat, in India to Afghanistan; a gold ram, a pair of small, ibex-like animals (Fig. 4.8; Potts 2012), and ivory combs. The combs, found near to or adhering to several skulls in the tomb at Tell Abraq, appear similar in design to combs that come from Central Asia or the Indus Valley; moreover, the ivory itself must have come from a region in which elephants are native (Fig. 4.9; Potts 2012). The settlement levels of Tell Abraq have also yielded three typical Indus Valley weights of the sort found by the hundreds at sites like Mohenjo-Daro, Chanhu-Daro and Harappa in Pakistan , and in smaller numbers outside the Harappan core area at Tell Abraq, Qalat al-Bahrain and Susa in southwestern Iran. Ceramics from southwestern Iran, Pakistan, Mesopotamia and Bahrain have been found as well (Potts 2012). It is possible that it was not the ceramics themselves that had value, but their contents: scholars have suggested the trade of pickled vegetables, dairy products, *ghee* (clarified butter), wine, honey and indigo at different points (Magee 2014, 112).

What does the presence of these foreign objects indicate? First and foremost, they signify the movement of boats across the Arabian Gulf. Excavations at the coastal sites of Ras al-Jinz and HD-6 (Ras al-Hadd 6) in the Sultanate of Oman by a joint French-Italian team have found more than 300 slabs of bitumen with impressions of bundled reeds, woven reed mats, or lashed wooden planks (Cleuziou and Tosi 1993), revealing important information about ancient boat-building construction of both reed-built and wooden-planked boats that traversed the waters of the Arabian Gulf. In a pioneering experimental attempt by a joint American-Italian-French project, information from the bitumen samples, data from cuneiform texts, iconography, and ancient grave-goods models, integrated with principles of naval architecture and engineering to build a viable sea-going vessel (Vosmer 2000). The built boat unfortunately sank soon after it set sail (University of Pennsylvania Museum of Archaeology and Anthropology, 2005), but it provided a great lesson in the complexity of ancient boat-building and demonstrated the need to learn more about these practices.

The foreign artefacts arriving on boats and eventually found in third-millennium BCE tombs were likely to have held important symbolic value in society at that time. Their presence suggests

4.8

4.9

Fig. 4.8–4.9. A pendant made of red gold showing two long-horned sheep and an ivory comb from the tomb at Tell Abraq.

that a certain segment of society benefited from increased exchange and trade with Mesopotamia and South Asia and may have emulated foreign elites through the display of prestige emblems (Magee, 2014). It is important to note, however, that these individuals were not differentiated in death.

Thus, the foreign objects confirm the important position that Tell Abraq maintained vis-à-vis international trade, although they do not indicate, as some scholars have suggested (see Edens 1992; During Caspers 1989) its dependence on exports from abroad.

Fortunately, the faunal remains from the excavations have revealed that this site had a flourishing subsistence economy, and its productive coastal fringe was the source of a realized reliable, year-round supply of marine foods.

Palaeoeconomy of Tell Abraq

The Tell Abraq faunal collection is by far the largest from any site of any period in Southeastern Arabia (Potts 1993, 188). Several thousands of identifiable animal bone, fish and shell remains have been found (Uerpmann 2001, 252), revealing important information about the subsistence strategies practiced at the settlement in antiquity. Domestic animals such as sheep/goat, and wild/ hunted animals and birds, such as gazelle, oryx, cormorant, turtle, dugong and dolphin remains have been found in abundance (Potts 2000, 61). The presence of high frequencies of a certain kind of shellfish, *Terebraliapalustris,* which were eaten in antiquity, indicates further that a mangrove swamp was probably located in close proximity to the settlement, since *Terebraliapalustris* are known to inhabit mangroves in large numbers (Fig. 4.10; Potts 2000, 64). The recovery of thousands of burnt date seeds in all levels of the site also confirms that dates were available at Tell Abraq and contributed in a large way to the inhabitants' diets (Potts 2000, 68). It is possible that some of these goods (remains of which are sometimes overlooked by archaeologists: like animal bones) salted fish, shellfish, sea turtle, along with imported goods from far-off lands, made their way to the inland oases, and were exchanged for cereals such as wild wheat, wild barley, domesticated two-row barley, six-row hulled barley, emmer and sorghum, which are

Fig. 4.10. Terebralia at a mangrove in Kalba.

Fig. 4.11. Ancient jawbone of an ungulate found at Tell Abraq.

known to have been grown at Hili 8, a third millennium inland settlement site in present-day UAE (Cleuziou and Costantini 1980; Cleuziou 1989, 79-80). However, evidence for fish and shellfish in the interior sites of the Arabian peninsula is rare (Magee 2014, 106). Animals operating as beasts of burden were essential for the maintenance of this intra-regional trade. Although the dromedary camel was not yet domesticated, it is possible that cattle were used for transport (Uerpmann and Uerpmann 2002). Magee also suggests that the role of the domesticated ass (*Equusasinus*) was probably an important development in this regard (Fig. 4.11; Magee 2014, 106).

Fig. 4.12. Softstone pendant from Tell Abraq.

Craft Production

A look at the ceramic traditions of the mid-third millennium BCE reveals further evidence of exchange between the foreign and coastal-inland areas of Southeastern Arabia. Mery (2013) and Potts (2005), in studies on the ceramic traditions in the 3rd millennium BCE, observe that the origins of ceramic industries are to be found in inland oases, such as at Hili 8, however, these vessel traditions appear to be inspired from the Indo-Iranian region, particularly from the Makran coast. Magee suggests that multiple waves of itinerant potters moved from different regions of the Indo-lranian region over the course of several centuries (2014, 106). The result according to Magee was a ceramic industry which, although located in the inland alluvial oases, served local funerary and domestic needs across the region (Magee 2014,108).

Additionally, softstone vessels and objects made from a workable metamorphic rock from the al-Hajjar mountains in the Oman peninsula (David 2002) dominate the funerary assemblage across the Arabian peninsula in this period (Fig. 4.12). The specific role of the vessels remains unknown; however it is likely they contained precious objects (Magee 2014, 109). They were also exported and were found in the Royal Graves at Ur and Tello in southern Mesopotamia, as well as Bahrain, Tarut, Failaka (Kuwait) and southern and southeastern Iran (Potts 1991).

Final Comments

The coastal location of Tell Abraq, as for many such coastal settlements in this period, provided its inhabitants opportunities to engage in maritime trade, exploit the readily available marine and estuarine sources for rich subsistence, and also connect to the inland for the distribution of foreign goods and copper, reflecting the dynamism that is characteristic of this period in Southeastern Arabia. Although archaeological and historical analyses focus on cultures that are bound by terrestrial conditions, there is also a maritime culture that enables inter-societal contact. The exploration of this maritime and coastal culture is therefore paramount in our reconstruction of ancient societies. It provides us with a renewed framework to imagine the coast-scape of not only Arabia, but also the Indian Ocean world — away from ideas of 'cores' and 'peripheries' that have for too long dictated archaeological and historical scholarship — and instead for the adoption of holistic, evidence-based approaches towards the past.

Coastal landscapes have provided easy pathways of movement along the shore edge, and between coast and hinterland, facilitating population migrations, cultural contacts, and relationships of trade and exchange for millennia. Interestingly, increased interdependence on trade and intertwined economies — the very forces that are driving the globalization of the world today — were contributors of the intensification of coastal development in the past. It is alarming that modern-day forces including dam building, coastal modifications, marine erosion, population growth, and rampant development, are destroying the very coastal sites that can tell us more about the niche that coastal settlements occupied in past societies (see Erlandson 2012, 140). What is more regrettable, perhaps, is that the history of coastal and seafaring societies from hundreds of thousands of years ago to the present, as well as countless sites that are of major religious, cultural, historical significance to communities around the world have not yet been recorded, excavated, or dated by archaeologists, and thus, their significance is unknown, making their protection a very challenging task.

Citing the exemplary progress and information that archaeological investigations in southeastern Arabia have been able to provide in such a short time as an example, it is apparent that there is an urgent need for countries of the Indian

Ocean to begin earnest efforts in survey, excavation and documentation of their rich coastal history. Project 'Mausam' aims to identify the lacunae that exist in the recording, documenting and preservation of the coastal landscapes of the Indian Ocean and encourage research that will help fill in these gaps. Such collaborations between governments and research institutions, as well as cross-disciplinary efforts, especially by integrating archaeology and history into contemporary coastal research (ecology, geography and land use studies) will enable a movement towards the protection of these highly threatened, yet critical sites that are an important part of our shared global cultural heritage.

Acknowledgements

The author wishes to acknowledge Prof. Peter Magee for his invaluable inputs on an early draft of this paper, and Rudi Vanzin for her helpful comments and suggestions.

References

Al-Jahwari, Nasser Said Ali, Settlement Patterns, Development and Cultural Change in Northern Oman Peninsula: A Multi-tiered Approach to the Analysis of Long-term Settlement Trends, Ph.D. diss., Durham University, 2008.

Bailey, Geoff, World Prehistory from the Margins: The Role of Coastlines in Human Evolution, *Journal of Interdisciplinary Studies in History and Archaeology* 1 (2004): 39-50.

Cleuziou, Serge, Excavations at Hili 8: A Preliminary Report on the 4th to 7th Campaigns, *Archaeology in the UAE* 5 (1989): 61-87.

Cleuziou, Serge and Constantini, Premiers Éléments Sur L'Agriculture Protohistorique De L'Arabia Orientale, *Paleorient* 6 (1980): 245-251.

Cleuziou, Serge and Maurizio Tosi, *In the Shadows of the Ancestors: The Prehistoric Foundation of the Early Arabian Civilization in Arabia,* Muscat: Ministry of Culture, Oman, 2007.

David, Helene, Softstone Mining Evidence in the Oman Peninsula and Its Relation to Mesopotamia, in Serge Cleuziou, Maurizio Tosi and Juris Zarins (eds.), *Essays on the Late Prehistory of the Arabian Peninsula,* pp. 317-35, Rome: Instituto Italiano Per L'Africa E L'Oriente, 2002.

Doonan, Owen, Sampling Sinop: Putting Together the Pieces of a Fragmented Archaeological Landscape, in Effie Fotini Athanassopoulos and LuAnn Wandsnider (eds.), *Mediterranean Archaeological Landscapes: Current Issues,* pp. 37-54. Philadelphia: University of Pennsylvania Museum of Archaeology and Anthropology, 2004.

During Caspers, E.C.L., Some Remarks on Oman, *Proceedings of the Seminar for Arabian Studies* 19 (1989): 13-31.

Edens, Christopher, Dynamics of the Trade in the Ancient Mesopotamian World System, *American Anthropologist* 94 (1992): 118-39.

Erlandson, Jon McVey, As the World Warms: Rising Seas, Coastal Archaeology, and the Erosion of Maritime History, *Journal of Coast Conservation* 16 (2002): 137-42. DOI 10.1007/s11852-010-0104-5

Frifelt, Karen, Evidence of a Third Millennium BC Town in Oman, *Journal of Oman Studies* 2 (1976): 57-67.

Magee, Peter, Eastern Arabia from 3000 to 2000 BC, in *The Archaeology of Prehistoric Arabia: Adaptation and Social Formation from the Neolithic to the Iron Age,* New York: Cambridge University Press, 2014.

Magee, Peter and Richard Carter, Agglomeration and Regionalism: Southeastern Arabia between 1400 and 1100 BC, *Arabian Archaeology and Epigraphy* 10 (1999): 161-79.

Méry, Sophie, The First Oases in Eastern Arabia: Society and Craft Technology in the 3rd Millennium BC at Hili, United Arab Emirates, *Revue d'ethnoécologie* 4 (2013): 2-16. DOI : 10.4000/ethnoecologie.1631

Potts, Daniel T., *The Arabian Gulf in Antiquity*, Vols. 1–2, Oxford: Clarendon Press, 1990a.

——, *A Prehistoric Mound in the Emirate of Umm a l-Qaiwain (U.A. E.): Excavations at Tell Abraq in 1989,* Copenhagen: Munksgaard, 1990b.

——, Rethinking Some Aspects of Trade in the Arabian Gulf, *World Archaeology* 24, 3 (1993): 423-39.

——, 'The Plant for the Heart Grows in Magan...': Redefining Southeastern Arabia's Role in Ancient Western Asia, *Australian Archaeology* 48 (1999): 35-41.

——, Marhashi and the Beginnings of Magan's Ceramic Industry, *Arabian Archaeology and Epigraphy* 16 (2005): 67-78.

——, *In the Land of the Emirates: The Archaeology and History of the UAE,* London: Trident Press and Abu Dhabi: Sultan bin Zayed's Culture and Media Centre, 2012.

Torben, C. Rick and Scott M. Fitzpatrick, Archaeology and Coastal Conservation, *Journal of Coast Conservation* 16 (2012): 135-36. DOI 10.1007/s11852-010-0121-4

Uerpmann, Margarethe, Remarks on the Animal Economy of Tell Abraq (Emirates of Sharjah and Umm al-Qaywayn, UAE), *Proceedings of the Seminar for Arabian Studies*, Vol. 31, Papers from the thirty-fourth meeting of the Seminar for Arabian Studies held in London, 20-22 July 2000 (2001): 227-33.

Uepermann, Hans-Peters and Margarethe Uepermann, The Appearance of the Domestic Camel in South East Arabia, *Journal of Oman Studies* 12 (2002): 235-60.

University of Pennsylvania Museum of Archaeology and Anthropology, Penn Museum Curator Gregory Possehl Sets Sail Beside the Re-created Reed Boat "Magan" Following Historic Trade Route Journey From Oman to India, Press Releases, 08 September. 2005, Accessed: 30 April 2014. http://www.penn.museum/press-releases/732-penn-museum-curator-gregory-possehl-sets-sail-beside-the-re-created-reed-boat-qmaganq-following-historic-trade-route-journey-from-oman-to-india.html

Vosmer, Tom, Ships in the Ancient Arabian Sea: The Development of a Hypothetical Reed Boat Model, *Proceedings of the Seminar for Arabian Studies,* Vol. 30, Papers from the thirty-third meeting of the Seminar for Arabian Studies held in London, 15-17 July 1999 (2000): 235-42.

Westerdahl, Christer, The Maritime Cultural Landscape, *The International Journal of Nautical Archaeology* 21.1(1992): 5-14.

5

The Coastal Temples of Vietnam: Sanctuaries of International Maritime Pilgrims on 'The Silk Road of the Sea'

Tran Ky Phuong

Between the 4th and 19th centuries a unique culture which owed its spiritual origins to Indian Hinduism developed on the coast of contemporary Vietnam. This is graphically illustrated by the remains of a series of impressive tower-temples located in a dramatic site that was the religious and political capital of the Champa Kingdom for most of its existence.

This is the description given on the UNESCO World Heritage site for the sanctuary of Mỹ S'on inscribed in 1999. The objective of this essay is to explain the cultural context of the site, including its maritime orientation. The discussion is divided into three sections: the first section presents a survey of the themes already covered in secondary writings; the second highlights the maritime connections of the Kingdom of Champa, while in the final part, I raise some of the issues to be addressed in the interdisciplinary Project 'Mausam' initiated by the Ministry of Culture, Government of India, that aims to explore the cultural heritage of coastal settlements along the Indian Ocean; along with various cultural dimensions of the monsoon winds that shaped communications and interactions across the seas.

Overview of Research

The kingdom of Champa in south and central Vietnam is often described as a federation of several units that had their own political centres. Its inhabitants lived both along the coastal plains and inland regions of Vietnam, and spoke languages belonging to the Austronesian (Chăm) and Austro-Asiatic language families. As a result, the art and architecture of the kingdom is often referred to as Chăm. The name of Champa appears for the first time in two Sanskrit inscriptions, one dated 658 CE, discovered in central Vietnam and the other dated 668 CE, found in Cambodia. Sanskrit and Chăm languages belong to two distinct language families and yet they co-existed in ancient Vietnam. Secondary writings often associate Chăm architecture with the modern nation state of Vietnam, yet historically, culturally and ethnically, the architecture spread beyond the present borders of Vietnam, over the upland areas of central Vietnam, extending into present-day Laos, Thailand and Cambodia (Fig. 5.1). The history of Vietnam is generally seen as the narrative of the two cultural groups, the Dai Viêt in the north, and the Chăm, believed to be of Malayo-Polynesian descent, whose temples spread over the coastal regions of south Vietnam (Sahai 2012, v).

Fig. 5.1. Map of Cham sites in Central Vietnam.

Inscriptions from the fourth to seventh century refer to the sacred Thu Bôn river as the Mahanadi or Ganga, one of the major rivers of

Fig. 5.2. The Holy Mountain named Mahaparvata or Mỹ S'on considered as a landmark of Amaravati Champa State in the north of the Kingdom. The mountain can be seen from the shore along the coast in Quang Nam Province nowadays. Mỹ S'on Sanctuary worshipped God Bhadresvara as the Father of the Kingdom, the protector of Cham sovereigns.

India; and the royal city in Trà Kiêu as Simhapura or Lion City. The two major sanctuaries of the Champa courts were Mỹ S'on in Quảng Nam Province, incorporating a complex of brick temple towers dating from the seventh-eighth to the thirteenth-fourteenth centuries (Figs. 5.2–5.3) and Po Nagar Nha Trang in Khánh Hòa Province dating from the eighth to the thirteenth centuries (Figs. 5.4–5.6). In the ninth century, Buddhist sanctuaries at Đông Du'o'ng were established, providing plurality to the art and architecture of the kingdom (Trân 2006, 3-6).

This religious architectural site was re-discovered in 1885 by a group of French colonial soldiers (Clémentin-Ojha and Manguin 2007).

Plan of Mỹ Sơn Site
(According to H. Parmentier)

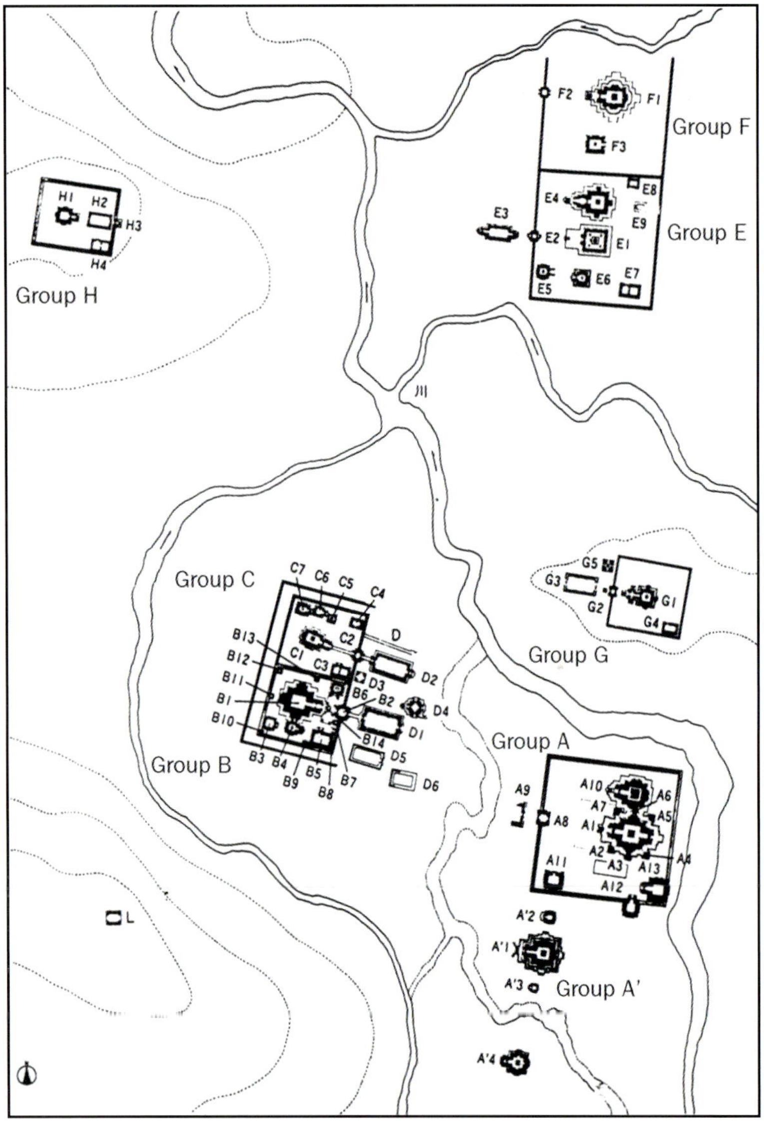

Fig. 5.3. Site map of Mỹ S'on Sanctuary. There are 68 ruins built from the 7th to the 13th century. (Map redrawn after Henri Parmentier).

Fig. 5.4. The temples of Po Nagar Nha Trang of Kauthara Champa State in the South of the Kingdom dedicated to Goddess Po Yang Inu Nagar, the Mother of the Kingdom. This sacred site was built on top of a hill near by an estuary. It was suggested that the temples were built for international maritime merchants who visited Champa Kingdom.

Ten years later, Camille Paris cleared the site from the jungle. In the years 1896-99, Louis Finot and Lunet de Lajonquiere came to Mỹ S'on to research the inscriptions found at the site. In 1901-02, Henri Parmentier researched on the art and architecture; and in 1903-04 along with Charles Carpeaux, carried out archaeological excavations at Mỹ S'on (Baptiste 2009, 14-25). The activities culminated in the year 1904, describing the research done on deciphering Cham inscriptions and remnants of Cham art found in Mỹ S'on, published in Bulletin d'Ecole

Française d'Extreme-Orient by Finot and Parmentier (*BEFEO* 1904, No. 4, 805-977).

In 1985, during the restoration works at Mỹ S'on B-C-D Groups, the archaeologists found a sarcophagus in rectangular shape made from several pieces of sandstone. It contained broken fragments of pottery and coal ash from a cremation. The sarcophagus was laid inside of a low wall between B6 and C3 towers. This is possibly the reburial tomb of a king who ruled around the 10th century, testifying to the fact that as well as a sanctuary for worshipping God Bhadreśvara (Śiva)—the tutelary of the kings, and royals' ancestor—Mỹ S'on was also a burial ground for the Cham kings (Trân 2008, 35-36).

The temples at Mỹ S'on have been subjected to human depredations and savage warfare in the twentieth century which have not only destroyed many of the structures, but also radically altered the nature of the entire complex. Under the aegis of UNESCO, restoration work of Group G monuments was done from 1997 to 2007 (Hardy, Cucarzi and Zolese 2009). Thus a history of conservation work done at the site needs to be factored into any future studies. This article is an attempt to comprehend the temple towers within the context of the cultural landscape as unearthed during archaeological excavations at several coastal sites (Figs. 5.7–5.12), as also to understand the inter-connections across the

Fig. 5.5. The statue of Goddess Bhagavati or Po Yang Inu Nagar, dated in mid 11th century, worshipped at the main temples of the site. She is still worshipped by local people nowadays as Mother of the Land.

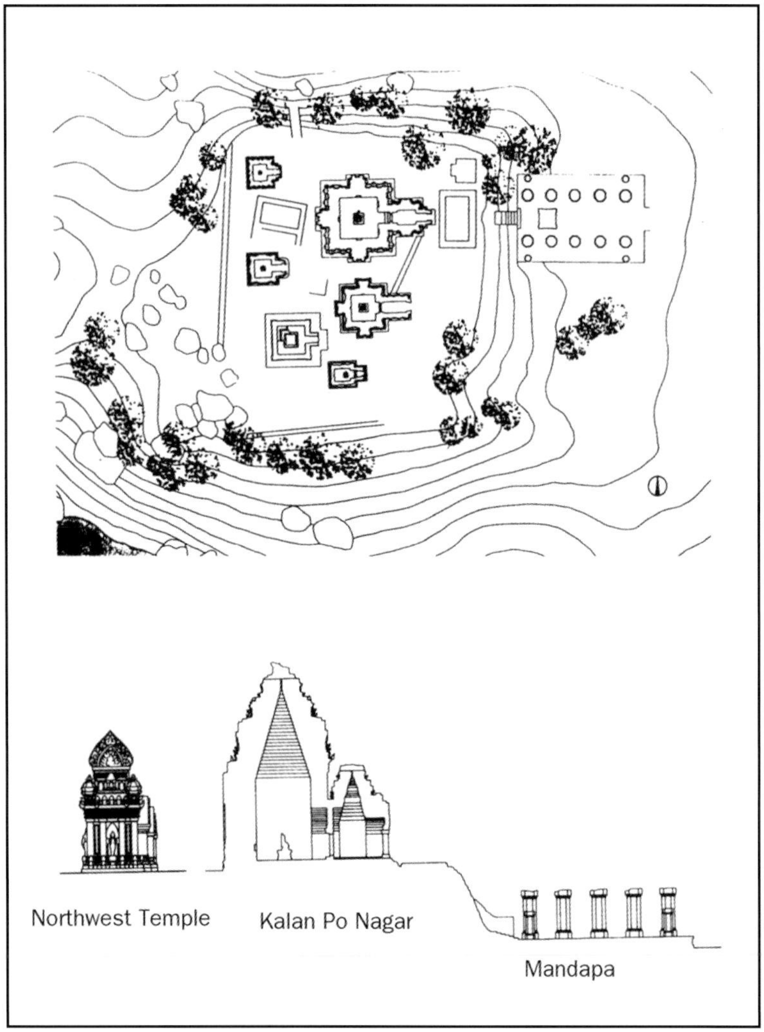

Fig. 5.6. Site map of Po Nagar Nha Trang Sanctuary. The temples of the site were built from the 8th to the 13th century. (Map redrawn after Henri Parmentier).

Indian Ocean, not only with centres in Southeast Asia and China, but further afield in South Asia.

Boats in the History of Vietnam

A somewhat different perspective emerges if the history of Vietnam is viewed from the vantage point of its 3260 kilometre-long coastline with two major deltas, i.e. the Red River delta in the north with its extensive agricultural plains and network of waterways and channels; and the Mekong delta in the south, which is low-lying, subject to flooding and best-suited for rice cultivation (Pham 2013, 137-68). The coastal plains are 50-120 kilometres wide and are bordered by the plateau of the Annamitic Chain on the west and the South China Sea on the east. Vietnam thus emerges as a land of wet-rice cultivation and fishing. It is no coincidence then that before the twentieth century, the waterways were the preferred means of transportation and the boat a critical element of the cultural life (Wheeler 2001). The Cham were not only experts in navigation over water but also in land transport trading slaves and aromatics. These skills helped them to attain a dominant position in the maritime trade of the South China Sea (Pham 2013, 151). This seafaring skill of the Cham makes it imperative that any discussion of their art heritage should also include an overview of maritime activities along the Vietnamese coast.

The history of the boat in Vietnam is not only a chronicle of trade and exchange, but also of

Fig. 5.7. The estuary as viewed from the site of Po Nagar Nha Trang.

warfare, often against neighbouring kingdoms. For example, the Bach Dang naval battle was won by the Vietnamese in 938 CE through a simple but ingenious tactic, through which the hero Ngô Quyên destroyed the powerful Chinese armada. The heavy and large ships of the Chinese are said to have been lured up the mouth of the river in the bed of which stakes had been planted,

Fig. 5.8. The Holy Mountain of Lingaparvata or Lingshan on the Ca Pass at Cap Varella as viewed from the Nhan Temple in Tuy Hoa City; the holy mountain was considered as the landmark of the southern state of Champa Kingdom. The mountain was noted in Chinese historical records from the 8th century.

invisible at high tide. When the tide receded, the small Vietnamese flotilla of light and easily manoeuvrable boats counter-attacked ferociously until the tide ebbed, impaling the enemies' ships on the stakes, blocking them in a forest of poles and enabling the Vietnamese troops to annihilate their enemies with burning arrows. The new Ly Dynasty (1012 1225) established the first Vietnamese state; the Dai Viêt or the greater land of the Viêt (Pham 2013, 148).

Dai Viêt participated in the on-going trade networks with Southeast Asia, China and India by developing harbours such as Van Don inaugurated in 1149, while the Cham harbours were located at Vijaya, Kauthara and Paduranga. Unfortunately there are few representations of Cham boats and only two undated carvings exist at Mỹ S'on and An Thinh quarry (Fig. 5.13). In contrast, it is often argued that the elaborate and graphic depiction of naval warfare on the walls of the twelfth-thirteenth century Bayon temple at Angkor shows a violent battle between the Cham and the Khmer. Bayon was the state temple of Jayavarman VIII and his successors, but is also perhaps "the most enigmatic and powerful religious construction in the world" (Freeman and Jacques 1999, 78). It is no surprise then that unlike other religious structures in South and Southeast Asia, graphic representations of naval battles find pride of place on temple walls. This engagement with the water and the sea was not unique to the kingdom of Champa, but was more deeply engrained in the preceding culture of the coastal polities, both Sa Huynh and Dong Son.

A study of the boat traditions of Vietnam shows that the narrative of power and ascendancy between the Dai Viêt and the Cham is not so linear, as often mentioned in secondary writings following a north-south axis but involved a larger ecological and cultural sphere. The beginnings of the history of the boat may be traced to the prehistoric period when both dug-outs and sea-

Fig. 5.9. The Nhan temple in Tuy Hoa City, Phu Yen Province. The brick temple, dated in the 11th century built on a hill near an estuary. The temple is close to the Lingaparvata Mountain on Ca Pass.

going rafts were used (Pham 2013, 139-41). There is evidence for the use of dugouts as boat-shaped burial coffins belonging to the Dong Son culture dated from 1000 BCE to 200 CE. To date, 171 boat-shaped coffins have been recovered from forty-four different waterlogged archaeological sites (Van 2005, 117-119).

Bronze casting in Vietnam emerged during the middle of the second millennium BCE and reached its peak around 500 BCE. The Dong Son ceremonial kettledrums decorated with beautiful intricately carved boat depictions are found in almost all of Southeast Asia, from north-east Thailand to Malaysia, to remote islands of Indonesia and as far as the Easter Island, suggesting an extensive network of seafaring activity. Seventy Dong Son sites have been found to date in a variety of environmental niches and

Fig. 5.10. The estuary viewed from Nhan Temple on the hill where the inscription of Cham King Bhadravarman in the 4th century was found.

are normally located close to rivers. Burials often in dug-out wooden boats were often located in separate cemeteries away from settlement areas (Su et al 2004, 117-208). From 111 BCE onwards, the Dong Son culture was encompassed by the Han and the region entered a phase of a thousand years of Chinese domination. It would nevertheless seem that the principal long distance

Fig. 5.11. The complex of Thap Bac or Silver Temple built in the 11th century, is located on a hill on the riverside that connected to the port city of Sri Boney of Vijaya Champa State during the 11th to 15th century.

Fig. 5.12. The Thoc Loc temple built on a high hill as a landmark of Vijaya Champa State in the 12th century.

carriers were the 'south sea people' or *Kunlun*, a term probably used for the maritime peoples of Indochina and later extended to the Indonesian population.

Contemporary with the Dong Son culture were the Sa Huynh sites, which appeared in a mature form around 600 BCE and continued into the first millennium CE in central Vietnam. The Sa Huynh Metal Age culture is named after an urn burial site close to the sea in Quang Ngai province, first investigated early in the twentieth century. These sites reveal a greater use of iron particularly for a variety of socketed tools and weapons, while bronze was used largely for decorative items. Another characteristic feature was the jar burial tradition with large lidded burial jars containing fragmentary human bones, small vessels, stone earrings and glass and carnelian beads. The material artefacts from the jar burial sites show evidence of interaction between the Sa Huynh and Han, Dong Son, Indian and other cultures (Bellwood 1992, 130-131). This participation in the wider maritime network of the South China Sea has continued throughout the centuries and extended as far as South Asia and further westward.

Fig. 5.13. A Cham sailing boat carved on the brick wall of Mỹ S'on B6 temple, dated in the 11th to 12th century.

The Maritime Network of Early Vietnam

The kingdom of Champa was situated on the great maritime routes called the 'Silk Road of the Sea,' which connected the two major Asian civilizations: India and China (Trân and Vu 1991, 17-24). Cham ceramics were known for their beauty and exported to large parts of the Indian Ocean world. Archaeologists have also unearthed several Cham ceramic kilns in former Vijaya state, located in present-day Binh Dinh Province. It is suggested that the temples indicate material affluence and that this is evident from archaeological work in central Vietnam that has revealed an urban landscape dotted with walled towns and citadels.

The kingdom's economy was based on maritime trade, which was facilitated by a network of wells that provided fresh water to Cham and foreign ships along the coast of Champa and the islands of Cu Lao Cham and Ly Son. The majority of Champa's export products came from the mountainous hinterland, sourced from as far as Attapeu in southern Laos. They included gold and silver, slaves, animal and animal products, and precious woods. By far the most important export product was eaglewood (Hardy 2009, 107-26).

Scholars often write about a boom in trading activity from the early tenth to the thirteenth century both in Southeast and South Asia, though data for these networks continues to be sparse and fragmented. From the ninth to the mid-fourteenth centuries, several merchant

Fig. 5.14. The Katu ethnic people, one of the strongest group of the Katuic speakers belonging to Mon Khmer language who live in the mountainous area of Quang Nam Province, formerly Amaravati Champa State. These people played an important role in providing luxury forest goods such as eagle wood, aloe wood, ivory, clover, spice, so on, for the Cham merchants in order to export to international markets in Central and East Asia.

Fig. 5.15. The Katu ethnic people still keep a strong tradition of their unique culture; they also maintain the oral history related to the exchange networks between the upland and the lowland in the region.

associations dominated economic transactions in peninsular India, such as the Ainurruvar, Manigramam, Nanadesi and the Anjuvannam. Associated with these merchant associations were communities of craftsmen such as weavers, basket-makers, potters, leather-workers and so on. The topographical distribution of the inscriptions is significant and they are clustered in the Dharwad-Bijapur and Mysore localities of Karnataka, while in Tamil Nadu larger numbers are found in Thanjavur, Tiruchirapalli and Madurai districts. Not only did these merchant associations develop powerful economic networks, but also employed private armies. They donated regularly to temples, which were at times named after them and also contributed to the construction of tanks (Abraham 1988). The range of their operations extended well beyond the boundaries of the Indian subcontinent into Southeast Asia.

Several clusters of Tamil inscriptions have been found on the eastern fringes of the Indian Ocean from Burma to Sumatra. Of the seven mid-ninth to late-thirteenth century Tamil or part-Tamil language inscriptions so far found in Southeast Asia, one has been found near Pagan in Burma, two just south of the Isthmus of Kra in the Malay peninsula and four in north and west Java. Perhaps the easternmost record is the bilingual Tamil and Chinese language inscription found associated with remains of one of the two Śiva temples at Quanzhou in south China. These inscriptions connect merchants associations operating out of south India with the founding or the endowing of temples or other structures for the use of the resident Indian merchant community.

This essay has established that along with the distinctive cult of the sanctuary, Mỹ S'on was one of the longest surviving historic sites in the whole region. It shows constant development of the architectural temple-towers from the late 4th to 19th centuries and this makes the sanctuary historically and archaeologically unique and significant for investigating within the framework of the Mausam Project, both for its architectural grandeur, but more so through its participation in the maritime networks of the South China Sea and the Indian Ocean (Figs. 5.14–5.15).

References

Abraham, Meera, *Two Medieval Merchant Guilds of South India,* New Delhi: Manohar, 1988.

Baptiste, Pierre, The Archaeology of Ancient Champa: the French Excavations, in Andrew David Hardy, Mauro Cucarzi and Patrizia Zolese (eds.), *Champa and the Archaeology of Mỹ S'on,* pp. 14-25, Singapore: National University Press, 2009.

Bellwood, Peter, Southeast Asia before History, in N. Tarling (ed.), *The Cambridge History of Southeast Asia,* pp. 130-31. Cambridge: Cambridge University Press, 1992.

Clémentin-Ojha, Catherine and Pierre-Yves Manguin, *A Century in Asia: The History of the École Française d'Extrême-Orient 1898-2006,* Paris: École Française d'Extrême-Orient, 2007.

Freeman, Michael and Claude Jacques, *Ancient Angkor,* London: Thames and Hudson, 1999.

Hardy, Andrew David, Mauro Cucarzi and Patrizia Zolese, *Champa and the Archaeology of Mỹ S'on,* Singapore: National University Press, 2009.

Hardy, Andrew David, Eaglewood and the Economic History of Champa and Central Vietnam, in

Andrew David Hardy, Mauro Cucarzi and Patrizia Zolese (eds.), *Champa and the Archaeology of Mỹ S'on,* pp. 107-26, Singapore: National University Press, 2009.

Pham, Charlotte Minh Hà, The Vietnamese Coastline: A Maritime Cultural Landscape, in Satish Chandra and Himanshu Prabha Ray (eds.), *The Sea, Identity and History: From the Bay of Bengal to the South China Sea,* pp. 137-68, New Delhi: Manohar Publishers, 2013.

Sahai, Sachchidanand, *The Hindu Temples in Southeast Asia*, Shimla: IIAS & New Delhi: Aryan Books International, 2012.

Su, Nguyen Khac, Pham Minh Huyen and Tong Trung Tin, Northern Vietnam from the Neolithic to the Han Period, in Ian Glover and Peter Bellwood (eds.), *Southeast Asia: From Prehistory to History,* pp. 177-208, Abingdon: Routledge Curzon, 2004.

Trân Kỳ Phu'o'ng, Cultural Resource and Heritage Issues of Historic Champa States in Vietnam: Champa Origins, Reconfirmed Nomenclatures, and Preservation of Sites, *Working Paper Series,* 75 (2006), Singapore: Asia Research Institute.

——, *Vestiges of Champa Civilization,* Hanoi: The Gioi Publishers, 2008 (Fourth Impression).

Trân Kỳ Phu'o'ng and Vu Huu Minh, ua Dai Chiem (Port of Great Champa) in the 4th-15th centuries, *Vietnamese Studies,* 2, 30 (1991): 17-24.

Van, Bui Liem, A Study of Boat-shaped Coffins from Dong Son Sites in Vietnam, *Indo-Pacific Prehistory Association Bulletin,* 25 (2005): 117-19.

Wheeler, Charles, Cross-cultural Trade and Trans-regional Networks in the Port of Hoi An: Maritime Vietnam in the Early Modern Era, Ph.D. diss., Yale University, 2001.

6

Heritage Routes and Gaps in World Heritage

Shikha Jain and Somya Johri

UNESCO and Heritage Routes

The concept of 'Routes' initially emerged and evolved as an idea of movement and dialogue in UNESCO between 1988-1994 when initiatives on the Silk Road expeditions and the Slave Road were launched as the 'Roads of Dialogue'. Other organisations such as the Council of Europe also began promoting this concept as the European cultural routes around the same time. UNESCO launched these two major programmes related to roads that connected the people of the world. The focus on the 'Silk Road' launched in 1988 was primarily to rediscover the linkages between the East and the West; the 'Slave Route' was launched in 1994 as a historical connection for Africa and the Americas. Other programmes launched along this theme for dialogue were the 'Iron Road' in Africa to look at the continental cultural context within Africa, 'Roads of the Al-Andalousi' for linking heritage between Europe, the Arab world and black Africa, 'Caucasus Project' for Europe and Asia, 'Arabia Plan', 'Intercultural Dialogue in Central Asia' and the 'Mediterranean Programme'.

Among these programmes, the two initial ones, i.e. the Silk Road and the Slave Route, continue as ongoing interactive platforms set up by UNESCO. The Silk Road project developed from 1987 to 1997 and the collected research data is now launched as a new online initiative, the Silk Road online platform, to compile and disseminate this valuable knowledge for the benefit of academic, cultural and artistic professionals as well as the general public. Moreover, the online platform continues the Silk Road's tradition and facilitates dialogue, encounters and exchanges among authorities, scholars, artists, educators, tourism professionals, students and youth. This initiative was launched with support of the Governments of Kazakhstan and Germany.

The programme of the 'Slave Route' has multiple objectives. It is a platform for research, publications and cultural activities concerning the Atlantic commerce, of counting and preserving files, of constituting databases, of promoting the improvement of school material, of establishing networks of researchers, and of supporting the development of the principal sites and of cultural tourism.

Routes on the World Heritage List

The idea of Routes as World Heritage Sites was initiated in November 1994 during the UNESCO Meeting at Madrid on 'Routes as Part of our Cultural Heritage'. When the Pilgrim's Route to Santiago de Compostela was added to the World Heritage list in Cartagena in 1993, Spain announced its intention of bringing together experts to discuss the question of 'cultural routes' in more depth. The World Heritage Committee approved this initiative at its meeting held in July 1994 in Paris. The expert meeting at Madrid recorded that "The concept of heritage routes is shown to be a rich and fertile one, offering a privileged framework in which mutual understanding, a plural approach to history and a culture of peace can all operate. It is based on population movement, encounters and dialogue, cultural exchanges and cross-fertilization, taking place both in space and time. The nature of the concept is open, dynamic and evocative, bringing together the conclusions of the global strategic study striving to improve the recognition within Heritage of the economic, social, symbolic and philosophical dimensions and constant and countless interactions with the natural environment in all its diversity".

This expert meeting at Madrid recommended member states to get involved in studies of such routes that will promote the spirit of the World Heritage Convention (*Convention Concerning the Protection of the World Cultural and Natural Heritage, 1972*) for collaborative conservation of universal heritage. Subsequently this idea was further explored in

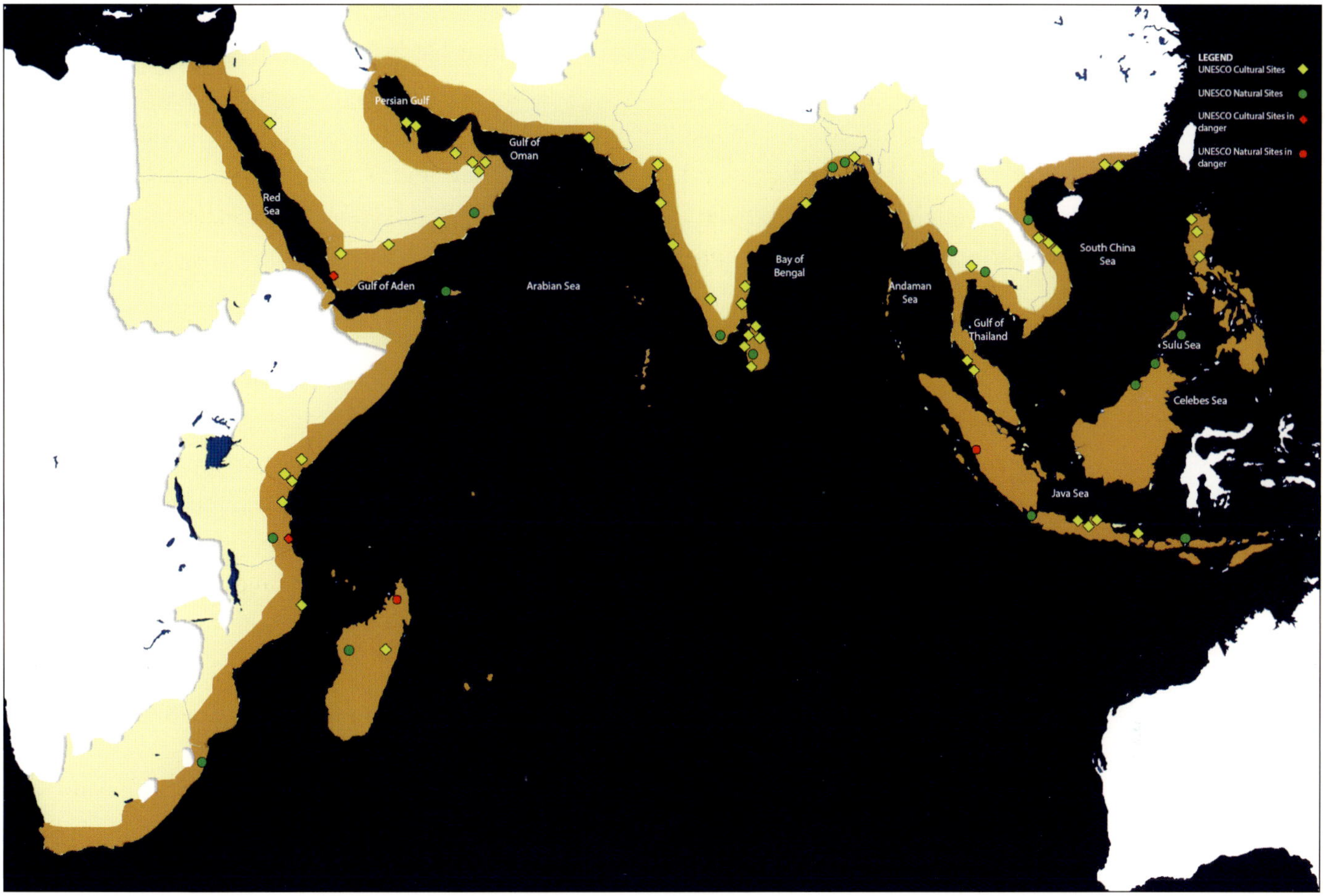

6.1 Map of Indian Ocean 'World' marking UNESCO's World Heritage Sites.

the following years and officially adopted by the World Heritage Committee in 2005 after experts and representatives of ICOMOS and World Heritage Centre drafted a series of proposals and guidelines to ensure the inclusion and proper management treatment of routes in the Operational Guidelines. The initial text of the Operational Guidelines was further revised a few times as per meetings and recommendations of the ICOMOS Scientific Committee on routes.

The ICOMOS Charter on Cultural Routes was adopted by the ICOMOS General Assembly in 2008. The most recent and updated version for nominating heritage routes on the World Heritage List as included in the Annex 3 of the Operational Guidelines 2013 is an abridged and slightly modified version of the text in this charter.

Meanwhile, with introduction of this new category in the Operational Guidelines, the member states took initiatives in this direction and proposed a number of routes—national and transnational—on their Tentative Lists which finally materialised in inscriptions as Pilgrimage Routes in the Kii Mountain Range (Japan, 2004) and Incense Route-Desert cities in the Negev (Israel, 2005). Besides these, ambitious transnational routes on the tentative list included Inca Roads in South Americas (2001-2003) and Silk Roads in China (2008), Kyrgyz Republic and Uzbekistan (2010), Kazakhstan (2012), Tajikistan (2013).

It is evident that the nomination of a transnational route involves exhaustive research and field surveys, is a highly complex process involving dialogue between several member states and is probably most challenging in terms of management and conservation than any other category of World Heritage Site. So, we should consider the most recent recommendation for inscription of the Silk Road sites on the Tian-shan corridor extending from China, Kazakhstan to Kyrgyz Republic as a benchmark achievement to be realised on the World Heritage List in June 2014. On the other hand, the dossier for the Penjikent-Samarkand-Polykent Corridor is proposed to be deferred which is disappointing for the member states of Tajikistan and Uzbekistan specially since years of research invested on the Silk Roads should have provided enough clarity for these member states on the site selection and comparative analysis.

There is no doubt that while the transnational route as a category is challenging in itself, the process of nomination makes it even more complicated. Despite recognition of routes on the World Heritage List and their inclusion in the Operational Guidelines, there are four primary concerns which still remain unaddressed:

a) Transnational routes are the most important category of World Heritage that reflect the collaborative spirit of the World Heritage Convention yet their definition remains confined as an Annex to the Operational Guidelines due to the limitations in the definition of 'Heritage' as per Article 1 of the original convention of 1972.
b) While there is some general consensus on description and characteristics of a

Heritage Route, the Operational Guidelines need to provide much more elaborate and precise instructions for member states.

c) There is no official recognition of this category on the World Heritage List so far and it is difficult to tabulate how many routes exist on the World Heritage List.

d) While ICOMOS recommended adoption of the term 'Cultural Routes' and accepted routes as primarily a cultural phenomenon (different from cultural landscape as decided in the ICOMOS General Assembly, Spain, 2002); the Operational Guidelines use the term 'Heritage Routes'. This will possibly allow us to acknowledge the impact of natural phenomena on routes in future.

As per ICOMOS Charter on Routes, 2008, the dynamic character of a cultural route does not obey natural laws or casual phenomena. It is true that the success of even the Maritime Trade routes was finally dependent on cultural factors and human endeavour, such as knowledge systems, spread of religion, building traditions and so on. However, it may be worthwhile to acknowledge the impact of monsoon winds that played a major role in facilitating sailing along certain sectors thus determining the passage of the route.

Gaps in World Heritage: The Maritime Trade Route in the Indian Ocean

With reference to the Global Strategy of 1994 aiming at a 'credible, balanced and representative' list and the gap analysis by ICOMOS and IUCN in 2004, new categories such as routes and cultural landscapes were supposed to bridge the gaps in the World Heritage List. Despite all good intentions of the World Heritage Committee, advisory bodies and member states in improving the balance, not much has been achieved to this end. The External Auditor's report of the 18th General Assembly of UNESCO records that categories such as 'routes' have led to further inscriptions of sites in countries which already had sufficient numbers in the World Heritage List rather than benefitting countries which have none or few properties inscribed. In such a scenario, maybe we need to review the perspective that guides these researches on the Routes. As already recorded in the initial report of the 'Silk Roads Project' by UNESCO, "these ancient roads, used for thousands of years and considered to have been 'opened up' by the Chinese General Zhang Qian in the second century BC, had no particular name. 'Silk Road' is a relatively recent designation dating from the mid-nineteenth century when the German geologist, Baron Ferdinand von Richthofen, named the trade and communication network Die Seidenstrasse (the Silk Road). The term, also used in the plural, has remained to stir our imagination with its evocative mystery." Maybe it is time for World Heritage to define, articulate and recognise universal heritage within its contextual framework rather than continue to look at it from myopic views of European Romanticism.

The Maritime Trade Routes in the Indian Ocean are undoubtedly one of the most significant routes in World History and definitely need to be celebrated on the World Heritage List. In previous studies undertaken by UNESCO, sections of this route may have been mentioned as 'Spice Route' or the 'Maritime Silk Route' which may remain as piecemeal approaches to the original routes if these are not studied within strong contextual historical setting of a series of transnational cultural landscapes and geographical context of the 'Monsoon phenomenon' and the 'Indian Ocean'. In order to explore these routes in totality, we definitely need to recognise these additional factors and understand the route in terms of the indigenous Arabian - Asian perspective beyond what has been researched and recorded till now.

Integrating the Existing List: The Maritime Trade Route in the Indian Ocean

The ICOMOS Charter on Cultural Routes, 2008 is quite extensive in identifying this category of heritage as an all-encompassing one thus allowing us to interlink existing sites on World Heritage and Tentative List in a wider framework of the macro narrative for a global route. It states that, "The consideration of Cultural Routes as a new concept or category does not conflict nor overlap with other categories or types of cultural properties—monuments, cities, cultural landscapes, industrial heritage, etc.—that may exist within the orbit of a given Cultural Route. It simply includes them within a joint system which enhances their significance. This integrated, interdisciplinary and shared framework creates new relationships among them by means of an innovative scientific perspective that provides a multilateral, more complete, and more accurate vision of history. This approach stimulates not only understanding and communication among the peoples of the world, but also increases cooperation to preserve cultural heritage."

An application of this approach on the existing World Heritage List reveals that 26 World Heritage Sites (Table 1) along the Indian Ocean coast in Africa, Arab and Asia region are already recognised for their Outstanding Value in contributing to maritime trade activities. While, an additional 17 sites (Table 2) have potential for being extended and recognised as outstanding coastal settlements under this theme. A large number of tentative sites along the coasts in these regions show great potential to add to this narrative and thus, a comprehensive research project focusing on the theme of Maritime Routes in the Indian Ocean would definitely enrich the World Heritage List in future.

As already recognised, the Routes provide an ideal platform for dialogue between nations and link various UNESCO Conventions under culture sector. The External Auditor's report at the 18th General Assembly which provides the future roadmap for World Heritage also emphasises on linking of conventions rather than just focusing on a single one for the listing of World Heritage. The suggested researches, publications, exhibitions, events, seminars, collaborations, training programmes under the Project Mausam being launched by India aims to achieve these objectives outlined for Routes under UNESCO. Additionally, the archaeological excavations along coastal settlements and underwater will contribute significantly in defining these routes as well as linking the World Heritage Convention with the convention on Underwater Archaeology.

Table 1. Existing World Heritage Sites across the Indian Ocean Region recognized for their Outstanding Universal Value in Maritime trade activities.

S.No.	SITE NAME	COUNTRY
AFRICA		
1	Island of Mozambique (*on Silk Route)*	Mozambique
2	Ruins of Kilwa Kisiwani and Ruins of Songo Mnara (*on Silk Route)*	Tanzania and Zanzibar
3	Stone Town of Zanzibar (*on Silk Route)*	Tanzania and Zanzibar
4	Lamu Old Town	Kenya
5	Aapravasi Ghat (*on Silk Route)*	Mauritius
6	Le Morne Cultural Landscape	Mauritius
7	Aksum	Ethiopia
ARAB STATES		
8	Al-Hijr Archaeological Site (Madâin Sâlih)	Saudi Arabia
9	Historic Town of Zabid	Yemen
10	Old Walled City of Shibam	Yemen
11	Tyre	Lebanon
12	Al Zubarah Archaeological Site	Qatar
13	Qal'at al-Bahrain – Ancient Harbour and Capital of Dilmun	Bahrain
14	Pearling, Testimony of an Island Economy	Bahrain
15	Land of Frankincense	Oman
ASIA AND THE PACIFIC		
16	Elephanta Caves	India
17	Sacred City of Anuradhapura	Sri Lanka
18	Old Town of Galle and its Fortifications	Sri Lanka
19	Ancient City of Polonnaruwa	Sri Lanka
20	Melaka and George Town, Historic Cities of the Straits of Malacca	Malaysia
21	Historic City of Ayutthaya (*on Silk Route)*	Thailand
22	Hoi, an Ancient Town	Vietnam
23	Complex of Hue Monuments	Vietnam
24	Historic Town of Vigan	Philippines
25	Kaiping Diaolou and Villages	China
26	Historic Centre of Macao	China

Table 2. Existing World Heritage Sites across the Indian Ocean Region with potential for being extended and recognized as outstanding coastal settlements under this theme.

S.No.	SITE NAME	COUNTRY
AFRICA		
1	Fort Jesus, Mombasa	Kenya
2	Sacred Mijikenda Kaya Forests	Kenya
3	Royal Hill of Ambohimanga	Madagascar
ARAB STATES		
4	Saint Catherine Area	Egypt
5	Archaeological Sites of Bat, Al-Khutm and Al-Ayn	Oman
ASIA AND THE PACIFIC		
6	Chhatrapati Shivaji Terminus (formerly Victoria Terminus)	India
7	Churches and Convents of Goa	India
8	The Great Living Chola Temples	India
9	Group of Monuments at Mahabalipuram	India
10	Sun Temple, Konark	India
11	Historic Mosque City of Bagerhat	Bangladesh
12	Archaeological Heritage of the Lenggong Valley	Malaysia
13	Borobudur Temple Compounds	Indonesia
14	Prambanan Temple Compounds	Indonesia
15	Cultural Landscape of Bali Province: the Subak System as a Manifestation of the Tri Hita Karana Philosophy	Indonesia
16	My Son Sanctuary	Vietnam
17	Baroque Churches of the Philippines	Philippines

References

All Answers Ltd, *Serial Transnational Cultural Routes on World Heritage List Tourism Essay.* http://www.ukessays.com/essays/tourism/serial-transnational-cultural-routes-on-world-heritage-list-tourism-essay.php#ixzz31PrIWkhg

Blair, Sandy (ed.), *Connecting Cultures and Continents: The Heritage of Routes and Journeys, Australia ICOMOS Historic Environment*, Volume 25, Number 3, 2013.

Carreño, Alberto Martorell, Cultural Routes: Tangible and Intangible Dimensions of Cultural Heritage, Scientific Symposium Main Theme, Place-Memory-Meaning: Preserving Intangible Values in Monuments and Sites, 27 - 31 October 2003, Victoria Falls, Zimbawe. 2003.

The ICOMOS Charter on Cultural Routes, 2008.

UNESCO, *Convention concerning the Protection of the Worl*d Cultural and Natural Heritage. *World Heritage Committee, Eighteenth session.* WHC-94/CONF.003/INF.13, Paris, 30 November 1994. Phuket, Thailand, December, 1994. http://whc.unesco.org/archive/routes94.htm

UNESCO, *Integral Study of the Silk Roads: Roads of Dialogue,* The Silk Roads Project, 1988-1997.

Zhou, Lv. Cultural Routes and the Network Construction of the World Cultural Heritage Conservation, 15th ICOMOS General Assembly and International Symposium: 'Monuments and Sites in Their Setting – Conserving Cultural Heritage in Changing Townscapes and Landscapes', 17 – 21 October 2005, Xi'an, China, 2005.

Contributors

Himanshu Prabha Ray is Chairperson of National Monuments Authority, New Delhi; Professor, Distant Worlds Programme, Ludwig Maximilian University, Munich and former Professor, Centre for Historical Studies, Jawaharlal Nehru University, New Delhi. Her research interests include Maritime History and Archaeology of the Indian Ocean, the History of Archaeology in South and Southeast Asia and the Archaeology of Religion in Asia. Her books on maritime contacts include *The Archaeology of Seafaring in Ancient South Asia*, Cambridge University Press, Cambridge, 2003, as also edited volumes, Satish Chandra and Himanshu Prabha Ray edited, *The Sea, Identity and History: From the Bay of Bengal to the South China Sea*, Manohar Publishers, 2013; H.P. Ray and E.A. Alpers, edited, *Cross Currents and Community Networks: Encapsulating the History of the Indian Ocean World*, Oxford University Press, New Delhi, 2007; H.P. Ray and J.-F. Salles, edited, *Tradition and Archaeology: Early Maritime Contacts in the Indian Ocean*, Manohar Publishers, New Delhi, 1996, updated edition 2012.
Email: chairperson.nma@gmail.com

Pravin Srivastava, IAS was Director-General of the Archaeological Survey of India and is Member-Secretary, National Monuments Authority. He has been earlier involved with the Archaeological Survey of India as Additional Director-General.
Email: directorgeneralasi@gmail.com

Yaduvir Singh Rawat trained in archaeology and is Director, Department of Archaeology, Gujarat State. He has explored and excavated a large number of sites in Gujarat. Email: ryadubir@gmail.com

Akshyeta Suryanarayan is Research Assistant, Indira Gandhi National Centre for the Arts, Janpath, New Delhi. She graduated from Bryn Mawr College, Pennsylvania, U.S.A in May 2013, with a double major in Classical and Near Eastern Archaeology and Anthropology. She has excavated at sites in Turkey, Jordan, United Arab Emirates and Sultanate of Oman as a student and as a trench supervisor, and plans to continue her postgraduate studies in Archaeology.
Email: mausamproject@gmail.com

Tran Ky Phuong has undergone archaeological training under renowned scholars in Europe. He has served as consultant UNESCO on World Cultural Museum Project, Academic Coordinator and Instructor for Council on International Education Exchange at CIEE Study Centre, National University of Ho Chi Minh City and various institutions in Vietnam. Besides, he has completed a number of fellowships in U.S.A., Singapore, the Netherlands, Malaysia and Japan.
Email: trankyphuong.cham@gmail.com

Shikha Jain is Director, DRONAH (Development and Research Organisation for Nature, Arts and Heritage), Chairperson DRONAH Foundation and Chief Editor of the biannual refereed journal *Context: Built, Living and Natural.* Her experience in cultural heritage ranges from steering conservation projects for various state governments to preparing conservation plans funded by international organizations such as the Getty Foundation, USA; World Monuments Fund and, preparation of Nomination Dossier and Management Plans for World Heritage Sites in India. She is also working on ADB funded projects on Urban Heritage for State Governments of Rajasthan and Himachal Pradesh. As a consultant to UNESCO, New Delhi, she worked on the Cultural Heritage Toolkit for JNNURM (Jawaharlal Nehru National Urban Renewal Mission), Ministry of Urban Development. Currently, she is also a Founding Trustee of the Indian Heritage Cities Network Foundation, a UNESCO recognised NGO and, a senior consultant to the Ministry of Culture, India serving as Member Secretary, Advisory Committee on World Heritage Matters.
Email: ms.acwhm@gmail.com

Somya Johri is a Conservation Architect from School of Planning and Architecture, New Delhi. She has worked with reputed organisations in India, involved in heritage conservation, such as DRONAH, CRCI and INTACH (Haryana Chapter). Recently, as a Senior Conservation Architect at DRONAH, she was in charge of projects such as Conservation Plan for Sheopur Fort, Madhya Pradesh for World Monuments Fund and preparation of Initial Assessment Reports of Heritage Structures in Punjab, a 13th Finance Commission Project with Government of Punjab. Currently, she is working as Project Manager, Project 'Mausam' and on the Advisory Committee on World Heritage Matters, Ministry of Culture.
Email: mausamproject@gmail.com.

Cover Illustration: Tanah Lot Temple at Bali, Indonesia (Photo by Somya Johri). The sixteenth century Tanah Lot is one of the seven sea temples built off the south-western coast of Bali on rocky outcrops within visible distance of each other. Legend associates the temple with Dang Hyang Nirartha, a priest from the Majapahit Kingdom in East Java who travelled to Bali in 1489 and is credited with the setting up of several shrines. The Tanah Lot thus represents an offshore structure that falls within the ambit of Project Mausam, even though it has not been discussed in any of the papers in this volume.